ABT

FRIENDS
OF ACPL

W9-AFR-181

SENSATIONAL SPORTS TEAMS
AMERICA'S TEAM
THE DALLAS COWBOYS

David
Aretha

MyReportLinks.com Books

an imprint of

Enslow Publishers, Inc.

Box 398, 40 Industrial Road
Berkeley Heights, NJ 07922
USA

MyReportLinks.com Books, an imprint of Enslow Publishers, Inc. MyReportLinks®
is a registered trademark of Enslow Publishers, Inc.

Library of Congress Cataloging-in-Publication Data

Aretha, David.
America's's team—Dallas Cowboys / David Aretha.
    p. cm. — (Sensational sports teams)
Includes bibliographical references and index.
ISBN-13: 978-1-59845-046-0 (hardcover)
ISBN-10: 1-59845-046-8
1. Dallas Cowboys (Football team)—History—Juvenile literature. I. Title.
GV956.D3A74 2007
796.332'64097642812—dc22

                          2006033824

Printed in the United States of America

10 9 8 7 6 5 4 3 2 1

To Our Readers:
Through the purchase of this book, you and your library gain access to the Report Links that specifically
back up this book.
The Publisher will provide access to the Report Links that back up this book and will keep these Report
Links up to date on **www.myreportlinks.com** for five years from the book's first publication date.
We have done our best to make sure all Internet addresses in this book were active and appropriate when
we went to press. However, the author and the Publisher have no control over, and assume no liability
for, the material available on those Internet sites or on other Web sites they may link to.
The usage of the MyReportLinks.com Books Web site is subject to the terms and conditions stated on the
Usage Policy Statement on **www.myreportlinks.com.**
A password may be required to access the Report Links that back up this book. The password is found
on the bottom of page 4 of this book.
Any comments or suggestions can be sent by e-mail to comments@myreportlinks.com or to the address
on the back cover.

Photo Credits: AP/Wide World Photos, pp. 1, 3, 6, 12, 14, 24–25, 28, 34, 36, 42, 51, 52, 61, 64, 71,
75, 76, 86, 92–93, 96–97, 99, 103, 106, 109, 113, 114; Ballparks by Munsey and Suppes, p. 79; Charles
Arey, p. 73; CNN/Sports Illustrated, p. 111; Dallas Cowboys, p. 82; databaseSports.com, p. 30; Doug
Drinen/Pro Football Reference.com; EmmittSmith.com, p. 55; ESPN Internet Ventures, pp. 59, 94; First
Base Sports, Inc., p. 31; Gerhard Peters — americanpresidency.org, p. 47; MyReportLinks.com Books,
p. 4; NFL Enterprises, LLC, pp. 11, 39, 57, 69; PFRA, p. 35; PLAYERS INC, p. 62; Pro Football Hall of
Fame, p. 88; Property of Dallas Cowboys Fan Club.com, p. 85; Scott M. Crevier, p. 20; SportingNews.com,
pp. 66, 101; SPRINGboard Agency, p. 46; Stadiums of the NFL, p. 81; Tank Productions, p. 26; The
SuperNFL, p. 48; The Texas State Historical Association, p. 19; The Washington Post Company, p. 17;
VikingUpdate.com, p. 45; World Almanac Education Group, Inc., p. 84.

Cover Photo: AP/Wide World Photos

Cover Description: Hall of Fame Quarterback Troy Aikman

CONTENTS

MyReportLinks.com Books
Great Books, Great Links, Great for Research!

The Internet sites featured in this book can save you hours of research time. These Internet sites—we call them **"Report Links"**—are constantly changing, but we keep them up to date on our Web site.

When you see this "Approved Web Site" logo, you will know that we are directing you to a great Internet site that will help you with your research.

Give it a try! Type http://www.myreportlinks.com into your browser, click on the series title and enter the password, then click on the book title, and scroll down to the Report Links listed for this book.

The Report Links will bring you to great source documents, photographs, and illustrations. MyReportLinks.com Books save you time, feature Report Links that are kept up to date, and make report writing easier than ever! A complete listing of the Report Links can be found on pages 116–117 at the back of the book.

Please see "To Our Readers" on the copyright page for important information about this book, the MyReportLinks.com Web site, and the Report Links that back up this book.

Please enter **DCF1448** if asked for a password.

COWBOYS FACTS

➡ **First Season: 1960**

➡ **Home Field: Texas Stadium**

SEASON	CHAMPIONSHIP	FINAL GAME
1970–71	NFC	Lost to Baltimore Colts, 16–13, Super Bowl V
1971–72	League	Defeated Miami Dolphins, 24–3, Super Bowl VI
1975–76	NFC	Lost to Pittsburgh Steelers, 21–17, Super Bowl X
1977–78	League	Defeated Denver Broncos, 27–10, Super Bowl XII
1978–79	NFC	Lost to Pittsburgh Steelers, 35–31, Super Bowl XIII
1992–93	League	Defeated Buffalo Bills, 52–17, Super Bowl XXVII
1993–94	League	Defeated Buffalo Bills, 30–13, Super Bowl XXVIII
1995–96	League	Defeated Pittsburgh Steelers, 27–17, Super Bowl XXX

RING OF HONOR	POSITION	SEASONS WITH COWBOYS
Troy Aikman	Quarterback	1989–2000
Tony Dorsett	Running Back	1977–88
Cliff Harris	Safety	1970–79
Bob Hayes	Wide Receiver	1965–74
Chuck Howley	Linebacker	1961–73
Michael Irvin	Wide Receiver	1988–99
Lee Roy Jordan	Linebacker	1963–76
Tom Landry	Head Coach	1960–88
Bob Lilly	Defensive Tackle	1961–74
Don Meredith	Quarterback	1960–68
Don Perkins	Running Back	1961–68
Mel Renfro	Defensive Back	1964–77
Tex Schramm	General Manager	1959–89
Emmitt Smith	Running Back	1990–2002
Roger Staubach	Quarterback	1969–79
Randy White	Defensive Tackle	1975–88
Rayfield Wright	Offensive Tackle	1967–79

Jay Novacek's 3-yard touchdown reception put the Cowboys ahead 10–0 during Super Bowl XXX.

TENSION IN TEMPE

1

For Super Bowl XXX, the people of Arizona rolled out the red carpet for the Dallas Cowboys. This star-studded team glittered like diamonds. They cruised the streets of Tempe in jewelry and limousines, and they stayed at a ritzier hotel than their rivals, the Pittsburgh Steelers. The world-famous Dallas Cowboys Cheerleaders served as their entourage.

And talk about talent! During this 1995–96 season, Emmitt Smith rushed for 25 touchdowns—then an NFL record. Cornerback "Neon" Deion Sanders sparked an electrifying defense. The 'Boys had breezed to victory in Super Bowls XXVII and XXVIII. Surely, this game would be another cakewalk for "America's Team."

But behind the glitter and neon, this Cowboys club had its troubles. Head coach Barry Switzer, who was often spotted rubbing his sore neck, had a whole set of headaches to deal with. He silently feuded with superstar quarterback Troy Aikman. Switzer had been fired at the University of Oklahoma because his team had lacked discipline. Aikman believed the same thing was happening in Dallas. How would the loosey-goosey Cowboys hold together against the Steelers, whose motto was PPP: Patience, Persistence, Physical?

Aikman himself was physically beat-up. His knees ached, and he would need elbow surgery after the season. Said Aikman on Super Bowl Sunday, "I've never been so happy for a season to end in my entire life."[1]

Dallas cornerback Larry Brown had endured a far more traumatic season. His son, Kristopher, was born prematurely in August, then died in November. "We didn't know what he was going through personally," said the Steelers' Rod Woodson. "All we knew was that he was hurting."[2] Key members of Dallas's mountain-moving offensive line were ready for retirement. Other Cowboys would leave as free agents after the season. Bemoaned Switzer, "We won't be as good next year as we are this year."[3]

Thus, when the Cowboys stormed into Sun Devil Stadium, the pressure was on. If they lost, in front of 750 million television viewers, they would be labeled "showboats" who failed to meet expectations. Meanwhile, in the backs of their minds, the Dallas Cowboy players knew that this could be their last Super Bowl ever. The pregame festivities featured a celebration of American Indian culture. Would *Indians* be a bad omen for the *Cowboys?*

From the start, Aikman proved his mental toughness. He marched Dallas into Pittsburgh territory, setting up a 42-yard Chris Boniol field goal. On the Cowboys' next possession, Switzer outfoxed the Steelers. He inserted the lightning-fast Deion Sanders (a defensive player) as a receiver. Aikman connected with Neon Deion for a 47-yard pass play. Aikman capped the drive with a 3-yard scoring pass to tight end Jay Novacek. After another Boniol field goal, the Cowboys led 13–0.

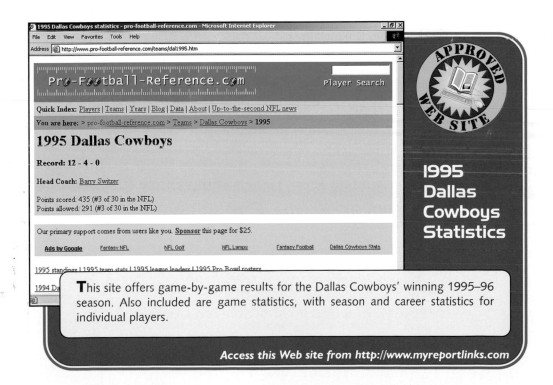

1995 Dallas Cowboys Statistics

This site offers game-by-game results for the Dallas Cowboys' winning 1995–96 season. Also included are game statistics, with season and career statistics for individual players.

Access this Web site from http://www.myreportlinks.com

At that point, the Cowboys were feeling pretty good about their chances. But the tenacious Steelers fought back. Quarterback Neil O'Donnell directed an impressive attack late in the first half. With thirteen seconds left, he connected with Yancey Thigpen on a 6-yard touchdown pass.

Both teams rested during a typically long Super Bowl halftime. (Singer Diana Ross left the field via helicopter after singing "Take Me Higher.") Cornerback Larry Brown knew he would see plenty of action in the second half. Since Sanders ranked among the NFL's greatest corner-backs, O'Donnell likely would throw in Brown's direction instead. Brown was ready for him.

In the third quarter, Brown intercepted an O'Donnell pass. He returned it 44 yards to the Steelers' 18-yard line, eliciting "wa-hoos!" from the Cowboy faithful. Aikman's 17-yard pass to Michael Irvin and a 1-yard run by Emmitt Smith put Dallas up 20–7.

On the next series, the Steelers turned the ball over on downs after Dallas stuffed Bam Morris near midfield on three straight plays. But from there, Pittsburgh roared back. With 11:20 left in the fourth quarter, Norm Johnson boomed a 46-yard field goal. The score was now 20–10. On the next play, Steelers head coach Bill Cowher pulled a bit of his own trickery. He called for an onside kick, and Pittsburgh's Deon Figures recovered.

O'Donnell drove his troops to the 1-yard line. Morris plunged in to make it 20–17.

After Levon Kirkland sacked Aikman, the Cowboys were forced to punt. The Steelers started their drive on their own 32. With 4:15 remaining, they were in position to win the game. Tension mounted on the Dallas bench. Should the Cowboys lose, it would rank among the biggest "chokes" in Super Bowl history. Switzer's reputation was already tarnished. A loss here could cost him his job and end his career.

But amid the pressure, a sole Cowboy emerged as a hero. O'Donnell fired into Brown's territory once more, and again the grieving cornerback picked him off. Brown snatched the ball at

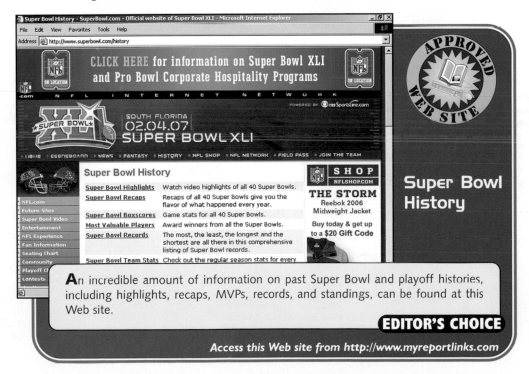

An incredible amount of information on past Super Bowl and playoff histories, including highlights, recaps, MVPs, records, and standings, can be found at this Web site.

EDITOR'S CHOICE

Access this Web site from http://www.myreportlinks.com

▲ Larry Brown races down the field after picking off a Neil O'Donnell pass.
Brown's key interceptions earned him Super Bowl XXX MVP honors.

Pittsburgh's 39 and ran it all the way down to the 6-yard line. Two plays later, Emmitt Smith ran in for a score, clinching a 27–17 Cowboys victory.

Coach Switzer loved a good party, and this one started when his players dumped a tub of Gatorade on his head. Switzer joined his Cowboys predecessor (Jimmy Johnson) as the only men to coach NCAA and NFL champions. Moreover, Aikman became the first quarterback to win three Super Bowls before the age of thirty.

But the hero of the day was Larry Brown. Before his tragedy, he had been heavily criticized. As a rookie in 1991, he had dropped numerous potential interceptions. In the NFC Championship Game a year before this Super Bowl, he was burned repeatedly by San Francisco receiver Jerry Rice. Unlike his flashy teammates, Brown was a quiet and humble player. But this day belonged to him. He was named the Super Bowl's Most Valuable Player.

"He's an amazing guy," said teammate Russell Maryland. "I don't know how anybody could go through the adversities he's gone through and still come out on top. God must have been looking down and gave him a hand."[4]

Aikman, Switzer, and company never would make it back to the Super Bowl. But they savored every minute of this exciting victory—and breathed a huge sigh of relief.

Cowboys General Manager Tex Schramm (left) greets coach Tom Landry at the airport on December 28, 1959.

AMERICA'S TEAM

2

Clint Murchison, Jr., had a mighty fat wallet. His father had struck it rich in the oil industry, and he himself ran a lucrative methane gas company. When the NFL wished to expand in 1960, Murchison stepped forward. He would finance a new team in his hometown of Dallas, Texas. There was, however, one small problem.

Owners of all the existing NFL teams had to approve the new club. Washington Redskins owner George Preston Marshall was the only man who threatened to vote against it. At the time, the Redskins were the only team in the South. Marshall believed that with a new southern team in the league his Redskins would lose support among those in Dixie.

That was when Murchison played hardball. He paid a large sum of money to composer Barnee Breeskin for the copyright to "Hail to the

Redskins," the team's popular theme song. Once he owned the song, Murchison threatened Washington's owner: If Marshall did not approve the Cowboys' admittance to the NFL, Murchison would not let the Redskins play their song. Marshall relented. He, as with all the other NFL owners, approved the sale. Thus began the legacy of the Cowboys—and their decades-long feud with the Washington Redskins.

⊜Building From Scratch

Murchison entered the football business with the proper attitude. Hire the right men to run the team, he believed, and then stay out of their hair. In retrospect, Murchison's selections were ingenious. He hired Tex Schramm as the general manager and Tom Landry as head coach. He also okayed Schramm's idea of hiring Gil Brandt as the team's top scout. Incredibly, this trio would run the Cowboys for nearly three decades, building the NFL's most successful franchise.

With the New York Giants, Landry had been the most respected assistant coach in pro football. He ran a tight ship, and he knew his Xs and Os as well as anyone. He was also exceptionally patient—a trait that came in handy in the Cowboys' initial season.

On September 24, 1960, thirty thousand fans assembled in the Cotton Bowl to witness the first game in Cowboys history. Movie star cowboy Roy Rogers and his horse Trigger arrived to entertain the fans in case the home team could not. Though the overmatched Cowboys led in the fourth quarter, the Pittsburgh Steelers came back to win, 35–28. The season went downhill from there, as Dallas finished 0–11–1 (0 wins, 11 losses, 1 tie).

A late-season tie with the New York Giants sparked only minimal fan interest. When the team returned from New York, two fans at the airport held a sign that said, "Well done, Cowboys." Landry looked at the two ardent supporters and

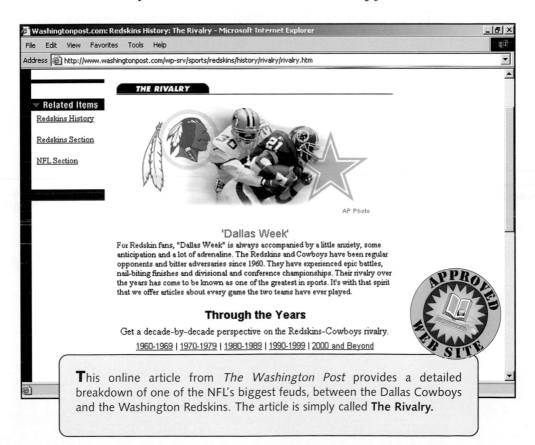

Washingtonpost.com: Redskins History: The Rivalry - Microsoft Internet Explorer

File   Edit   View   Favorites   Tools   Help

Address http://www.washingtonpost.com/wp-srv/sports/redskins/history/rivalry/rivalry.htm

THE RIVALRY

Related Items

Redskins History

Redskins Section

NFL Section

AP Photo

'Dallas Week'

For Redskin fans, "Dallas Week" is always accompanied by a little anxiety, some anticipation and a lot of adrenaline. The Redskins and Cowboys have been regular opponents and bitter adversaries since 1960. They have experienced epic battles, nail-biting finishes and divisional and conference championships. Their rivalry over the years has come to be known as one of the greatest in sports. It's with that spirit that we offer articles about every game the two teams have ever played.

Through the Years

Get a decade-by-decade perspective on the Redskins-Cowboys rivalry.

1960-1969 | 1970-1979 | 1980-1989 | 1990-1999 | 2000 and Beyond

APPROVED WEB SITE

This online article from *The Washington Post* provides a detailed breakdown of one of the NFL's biggest feuds, between the Dallas Cowboys and the Washington Redskins. The article is simply called **The Rivalry.**

said to Schramm, "Looks like we're making some progress."[1]

→ Dandy Don and Bullet Bob

On opening day 1961, Dallas celebrated its first-ever victory. Allen Green booted a 24-yard field goal to defeat Pittsburgh 27–24. From 1961 to 1965, the Cowboys failed to post a winning record. Fans urged the team to fire Landry. However, the Cowboys believed they were building a strong foundation, and they re-signed their head coach to a ten-year contract.

Gil Brandt drafted wisely, beginning with defensive terror Bob Lilly in 1961. Running back Don Perkins slithered through holes for big gains. Mel Renfro picked off passes like cherries off a tree. Receiver Bob Hayes, the "World's Fastest Human," electrified the Cotton Bowl with his game-breaking plays. Finally, with swashbuckling "Dandy" Don Meredith at quarterback, Dallas broke through in 1966.

The Cowboys opened the 1966 season at 4–0. In a 56–7 rout of Philadelphia, Meredith threw 5 touchdown passes—including 3 to "Bullet Bob" Hayes. Against Atlanta, linebacker Chuck Howley rumbled 97 yards to paydirt. In their first-ever Thanksgiving Day game (which would become a Cowboys tradition), Dallas stuffed Cleveland like a turkey. With a record of 10–3–1, Dallas earned a

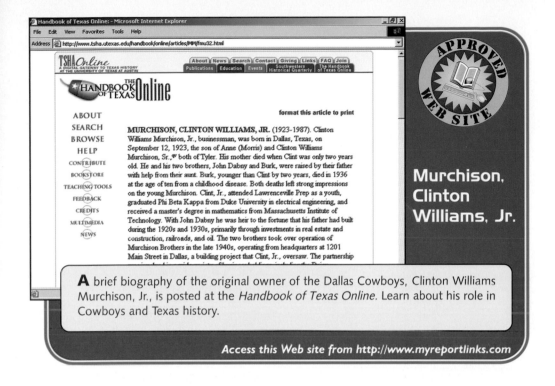

A brief biography of the original owner of the Dallas Cowboys, Clinton Williams Murchison, Jr., is posted at the *Handbook of Texas Online.* Learn about his role in Cowboys and Texas history.

Access this Web site from http://www.myreportlinks.com

spot in the NFL Championship Game against the Green Bay Packers.

Cowboy fans were ecstatic. The title game took place at the Cotton Bowl, and tickets were sold out the morning they went on sale. Green Bay took a 34–20 lead, but Meredith led a fourth-quarter comeback. First he connected with Frank Clarke for a 68-yard touchdown, making it 34–27. He then drove Dallas to the 1-yard line with less than two minutes to go. On fourth down, the Cowboys tried the play "Fire 90 Quarterback Roll Right." Meredith rolled right and fired—right into the hands of the Packers' Tom Brown. Green Bay won the NFL championship, and advanced to the inaugural Super Bowl against the American Football League (AFL) champion Kansas City Chiefs.

→The Ice Bowl

During the 1967 preseason, the Cowboys hosted Green Bay in sweltering Texas heat. With the temperature well into the 90s and the humidity oppressive, the players longed for cooler weather. As the saying goes: Be careful what you wish for.

Dallas went 9–5 in 1967 and crushed Cleveland, 52–14, in the opening playoff game. That set up an NFL Championship Game rematch with Green Bay. The winner would go to the Super Bowl against the champion of the AFL,

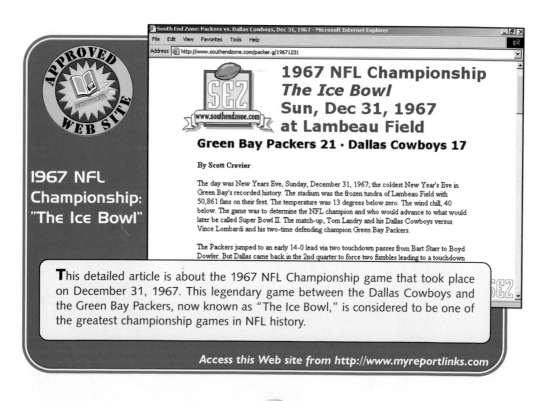

APPROVED WEB SITE

1967 NFL Championship: "The Ice Bowl"

South End Zone: Packers vs. Dallas Cowboys, Dec 31, 1967 - Microsoft Internet Explorer

File   Edit   View   Favorites   Tools   Help

Address http://www.southendzone.com/packer.g/19671231

www.southendzone.com

1967 NFL Championship
The Ice Bowl
Sun, Dec 31, 1967
at Lambeau Field
Green Bay Packers 21 · Dallas Cowboys 17

By Scott Crevier

The day was New Years Eve, Sunday, December 31, 1967; the coldest New Year's Eve in Green Bay's recorded history. The stadium was the frozen tundra of Lambeau Field with 50,861 fans on their feet. The temperature was 13 degrees below zero. The wind chill, 40 below. The game was to determine the NFL champion and who would advance to what would later be called Super Bowl II. The match-up, Tom Landry and his Dallas Cowboys versus Vince Lombardi and his two-time defending champion Green Bay Packers.

The Packers jumped to an early 14-0 lead via two touchdown passes from Bart Starr to Boyd Dowler. But Dallas came back in the 2nd quarter to force two fumbles leading to a touchdown

This detailed article is about the 1967 NFL Championship game that took place on December 31, 1967. This legendary game between the Dallas Cowboys and the Green Bay Packers, now known as "The Ice Bowl," is considered to be one of the greatest championship games in NFL history.

Access this Web site from http://www.myreportlinks.com

the Oakland Raiders. To get there, however, both teams had to weather a frozen hell.

The Packers hosted the Cowboys at Lambeau Field in Green Bay on December 31. At game time, the temperature read 13 degrees below zero, with windchill readings dropping to 48 degrees below. Coffee, toilets, and reporters' typewriters all froze.

Accustomed to cold weather, the Packers went ahead 14–0. However, Dallas took advantage of Green Bay fumbles and led 17–14 with 4:50 remaining. By that time, the temperature plummeted to 18 degrees below zero. The field was a sheet of ice. With sixteen seconds left, the Packers had the ball on the Dallas 1-yard line. Quarterback Bart Starr plunged in for a touchdown, and the Packers won the "Ice Bowl" 21–17.

Cannot Win the Big One

The Cowboys remained a powerhouse in 1968. They started 6–0, finished 12–2, and scored an NFL-high 431 points (including 59 on Opening Day). However, two losses proved significant. Dallas lost a regular season rematch to Green Bay. Then came a bitter loss in the playoffs at Cleveland. Dallas was so heavily favored that "if we win by only one touchdown," said a Cowboy, "it will be a bad day."[2] They lost 31–20.

A new era began for Dallas in 1969. Quarterback Don Meredith and running back Don

Perkins—each a Pro Bowler from 1966 through 1968—retired. But the offense did not skip a beat. Craig Morton, with his flattop haircut, took over as starting quarterback. Calvin Hill, a rookie from Yale University, ran for 942 yards. Dallas finished 11–2–1—only to get routed by Cleveland 38–14 in the opening playoff game.

For the fourth consecutive year, the Cowboys had blown the season in the playoffs. Throughout America, they were known as the talented team that could not win the big one. "I just don't know what it is," said frustrated Cowboys star Bob Lilly. "That's the toughest part of all. We don't know the answer."[3]

The answer came in 1970 in the form of the "Doomsday Defense."

⊛Tough D and the "Blooper Bowl"

For years, the Cowboys defense had boasted such "studs" as defensive lineman Bob Lilly and linebackers Lee Roy Jordan and Chuck Howley. In 1970, they added a pair of rookie defensive backs who would give receivers fits: Cliff Harris and Charlie Waters. Dallas opened 1970 at a modest 5–4. However, they won their last five games, winning by such one-sided scores as 16–3, 34–0, and 52–10.

The Doomsday Defense so dominated Detroit in the opening playoff game that the Cowboys prevailed by the score of 5–0. Two points came on a safety—a sack in the end zone. In the NFC Championship Game, Dallas defused the explosive offense of the San Francisco 49ers. The 'Boys prevailed 17–10. For the first time in team history, they were off to the Super Bowl.

Conditions at the Orange Bowl in Miami were perfect: 70°F and sunny. But the game between Dallas and the Baltimore Colts became known as the "Blooper Bowl," as the teams combined for 11 turnovers. Dallas could have gone up 19–6 in the second half, but rookie Duane Thomas fumbled the ball at Baltimore's 2-yard line. The Colts came back to win 16–13. Wrote Tex Maule of *Sports Illustrated*, "Both teams blundered through a laugher of a Super Bowl, but in the end the joke was on the Cowboys, who made the biggest mistake of all—losing."[4]

Champs at Last

In 1971, the Cowboys finally earned first-class status. They moved out of the dilapidated Cotton Bowl and into the $35 million Texas Stadium. Former President Lyndon Johnson attended the first game on October 24. Roger Staubach emerged as the team's No. 1 quarterback. The former Navy star possessed a rocket arm, quick feet, and the leadership skills to steer the ship. Behind "Roger the Dodger," Dallas won its last seven

Lee Roy Jordan, No. 55, leads the charge as the Cowboys defense swarms Eagles receiver Harold Carmichael on November 15, 1971.

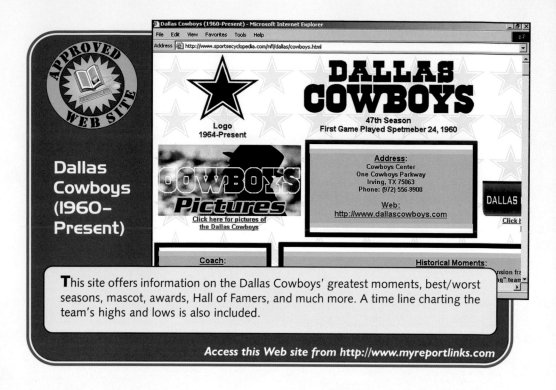

Dallas Cowboys (1960– Present)

This site offers information on the Dallas Cowboys' greatest moments, best/worst seasons, mascot, awards, Hall of Famers, and much more. A time line charting the team's highs and lows is also included.

Access this Web site from http://www.myreportlinks.com

games and rolled past Minnesota and San Francisco in the playoffs.

Super Bowl VI took place in New Orleans, where the game-time temperature was a brisk 39°F. Coach Landry emphasized his "KISS" strategy: Keep It Simple, Stupid. Determined to lose their "chokers" label, the Cowboys went out and harpooned the Miami Dolphins.

In the second and third quarters, Staubach masterfully led two eight-play drives—both in excess of 70 yards. Lance Alworth scored on a 7-yard pass, and Duane Thomas romped in for a 3-yard score. Staubach's fourth-quarter TD pass to tight end Mike Ditka made the score 24–3, and that was how it ended. It is the only Super Bowl in history in which one of the teams did not score a touchdown.

After the game, the Cowboys felt more "relieved" than anything, said linebacker Lee Roy Jordan. "[I]t was certainly a great thrill, but for us, it was more of a lifting of a heavy burden that we had been bearing since 1966. . . . It was almost anticlimactic—it was more important to get the bridesmaid-but-never-a-bride tag removed from us."[5]

With that tag completely ripped off, the Cowboys proceeded to build one of the greatest dynasties in NFL history.

⊜ Cheers, Prayers, and Comebacks

The Cowboys cruised through the 1972 season with a 10–4 record, but the real drama occurred in their first playoff game against San Francisco. Down 28–16, Staubach fired a touchdown pass with 1:30 left in the game. Incredibly, Dallas recovered an onside kick and scored again on a pass to receiver Ron Sellers. Staubach—"Captain Comeback"—led his troops to a 30–28 triumph. The next week, however, Washington trounced the Cowboys 26–3.

The Cowboys duplicated their 10–4 record in 1973 and beat the Los Angeles Rams in the playoffs. But they once again lost the NFC Championship Game, falling to Minnesota 27–10.

▲ Head Coach Tom Landry is carried off the field as the Cowboys celebrate their victory in Super Bowl VI. The players pictured are Bob Hayes (No. 22), Rayfield Wright (No. 70), and Mel Renfro (No. 20).

Around this time, the Dallas Cowboys Cheerleaders started to catch the nation's attention. The young women were athletic, talented, and attractive. Their "cowgirl" outfits could not get any skimpier. In 1979, the TV movie *The Dallas Cowboys Cheerleaders* would be a ratings smash. All the while, women's rights activists criticized the cheerleaders as being poor role models for girls.

Super Bowl X

After an 8–6 campaign in 1974, the Cowboys bounced back with seven straight seasons with at least ten wins. In the first round of the 1975 playoffs, Staubach defeated Minnesota on a memorable "Hail Mary" pass. With thirty-six seconds remaining and Dallas down 14–10, Staubach heaved a desperation pass toward the goal line. "I closed my eyes and said a Hail Mary," Staubach explained.[6] Wide receiver Drew Pearson hauled it in for the winning score.

Dallas blew out Los Angeles 37–7 the next week and returned to the Super Bowl against the mighty Steelers. Pittsburgh's "Steel Curtain" defense, led by "Mean" Joe Greene, sent eight defenders to the Pro Bowl that season. The Cowboys boasted their own powerful D, including six-foot nine-inch lineman Ed "Too Tall" Jones.

The outcome of this game hinged on one pivotal play. With 4:25 left in the game, Pittsburgh

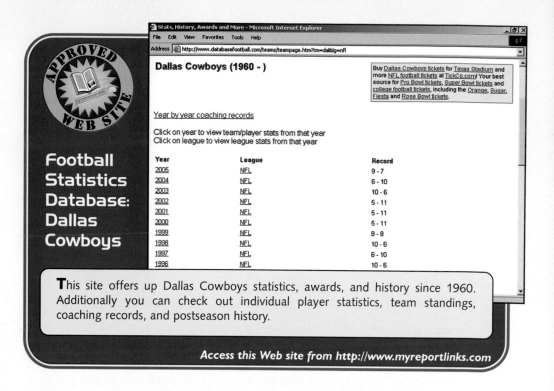

Stats, History, Awards and More - Microsoft Internet Explorer

File   Edit   View   Favorites   Tools   Help

Address http://www.databasefootball.com/teams/teampage.htm?tm=dal&lg=nfl

Dallas Cowboys (1960 -)

Buy Dallas Cowboys tickets for Texas Stadium and more NFL football tickets at TickCo.com! Your best source for Pro Bowl tickets, Super Bowl tickets and college football tickets, including the Orange, Sugar, Fiesta and Rose Bowl tickets.

Year by year coaching records

Click on year to view team/player stats from that year
Click on league to view league stats from that year

Year	League	Record
2005	NFL	9 - 7
2004	NFL	6 - 10
2003	NFL	10 - 6
2002	NFL	5 - 11
2001	NFL	5 - 11
2000	NFL	5 - 11
1999	NFL	8 - 8
1998	NFL	10 - 6
1997	NFL	6 - 10
1996	NFL	10 - 6

Football Statistics Database: Dallas Cowboys

This site offers up Dallas Cowboys statistics, awards, and history since 1960. Additionally you can check out individual player statistics, team standings, coaching records, and postseason history.

Access this Web site from http://www.myreportlinks.com

led 15–10. The Steelers had the ball, but they faced third down and six on their own 36-yard line. Safety Cliff Harris blitzed and nailed quarterback Terry Bradshaw immediately after he unloaded a long bomb. Lynn Swann caught the pass for a touchdown, while Bradshaw left with a head injury. After a missed extra point, Pittsburgh led 21–10.

Dallas rallied with a Staubach to Percy Howard touchdown pass, and with 1:12 remaining, the Cowboys got the ball back. However, the Steel Curtain closed on Dallas. Glen Edwards intercepted a pass in the end zone, concluding one of the most exciting Super Bowls ever played.

→ Orange Crushed

The Cowboys finished 11–3 in 1976 but were upset by the Rams 14–12 in the opening playoff game. In 1977, however, Dallas boasted its greatest team yet. Rookie Tony Dorsett rushed for 1,007 yards, sparking the second best offense in the NFL. Linebacker Thomas "Hollywood" Henderson—who could slam-dunk the ball over the crossbar after a touchdown—added pizzazz. The Cowboys went 12–2 and then "mopped the floor" with Chicago and Minnesota in the playoffs. The Cowboys were big favorites against the 12–2 Denver Broncos in the Super Bowl, and they delivered.

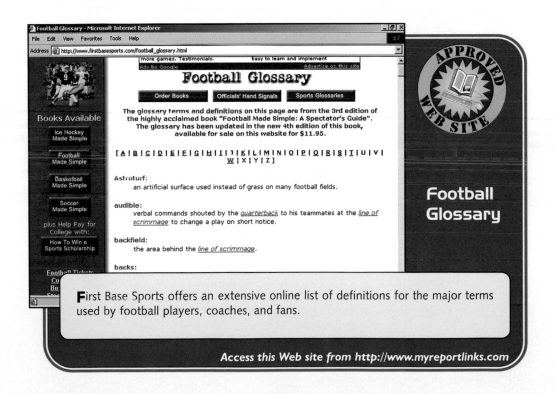

First Base Sports offers an extensive online list of definitions for the major terms used by football players, coaches, and fans.

Access this Web site from http://www.myreportlinks.com

Denver was known for its "Orange Crush" defense, but it was the Cowboys D that did the squashing. In the first half, Dallas forced seven turnovers and took a 13–0 lead. In the third quarter, Butch Johnson made a fingertip catch for a 45-yard touchdown. The extra point made it 20–3, and Dallas cruised 27–10. The Dallas defense was so dominant that two Cowboys defenders were voted Super Bowl co-MVPs: defensive linemen Randy White and Harvey Martin.

Too Much Trash Talk

The Cowboys brimmed with so much talent in 1978 that some predicted the team would go undefeated. They were so dynamic and appealing that they had become known as "America's Team." On *Monday Night Football* in September, they ran up 583 yards in a 38–0 trouncing of Baltimore. Dallas finished 12–4 while totaling the most points scored and allowing the third fewest points in the NFL. After cruising past Atlanta and shutting out the Los Angeles Rams in the playoffs, Dallas returned to the Super Bowl for a record-setting fifth time.

The matchup between the Cowboys and Steelers provided the most anticipated Super Bowl yet. Each team had won two Super Bowls in the 1970s, and the winner would be recognized as the "team of the decade." Dallas linebacker

Hollywood Henderson may have doomed the Cowboys with his inflammatory trash talk. Henderson claimed that Pittsburgh quarterback Terry Bradshaw "couldn't spell *cat* if you spotted him the *c* and the *a*."[7]

Bradshaw hated having his intelligence questioned, and he took out his anger on the Cowboys. In the first half, he rifled 3 touchdown passes to give Pittsburgh a 21–14 halftime lead. Dallas could have tied the score in the third quarter, but a wide-open Jackie Smith dropped a certain touchdown pass in the end zone. A field goal made it 21–17.

The Steelers moved ahead 35–17 before Staubach launched one of his patented comebacks. Staubach threw a 7-yard touchdown pass to Billy Joe Dupree with just over two minutes left. After recovering an onside kick, Staubach fired another scoring pass. However, the Steelers recovered another Cowboys onside kick to preserve a 35–31 victory. Bradshaw, with 4 touchdown passes, had no trouble spelling MVP.

⊝ One Last Hurrah

In 1979, it was clear that the Cowboys were fading. Ed "Too Tall" Jones quit to take up boxing, and Roger Staubach contemplated retirement. However, he still had one great comeback left in him.

In the last game of the regular season, Staubach orchestrated two long touchdown drives in the last four minutes. After a lob pass to Tony Hill in the end zone, and the extra point, Dallas won 35–34. Staubach called it "a game like no

▲ Ed "Too Tall" Jones struts off the field after sacking Broncos quarterback Craig Morton.

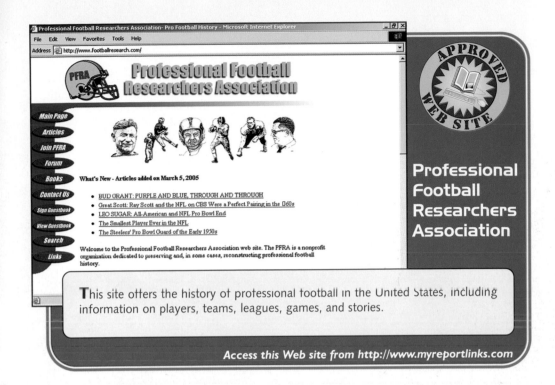

Professional Football Researchers Association- Pro Football History - Microsoft Internet Explorer

File   Edit   View   Favorites   Tools   Help

Address http://www.footballresearch.com/

Professional Football Researchers Association

Main Page
Articles
Join PFRA
Forum
Books
Contact Us
Sign Guestbook
View Guestbook
Search
Links

What's New - Articles added on March 5, 2005

- BUD GRANT: PURPLE AND BLUE, THROUGH AND THROUGH
- Great Scott: Ray Scott and the NFL on CBS Were a Perfect Pairing in the 060s
- LEO SUGAR: All-American and NFL Pro Bowl End
- The Smallest Player Ever in the NFL
- The Steelers' Pro Bowl Guard of the Early 1950s

Welcome to the Professional Football Researchers Association web site. The PFRA is a nonprofit organization dedicated to preserving and, in some cases, reconstructing professional football history.

Professional Football Researchers Association

This site offers the history of professional football in the United States, including information on players, teams, leagues, games, and stories.

Access this Web site from http://www.myreportlinks.com

other . . . absolutely the most thrilling 60 minutes I ever spent on a football field."[8] It was also his last career victory. In the first round of the play-offs, the Cowboys lost to the Los Angeles Rams 21–19.

The hit show on television during that 1979 season was *Dallas,* and *Dynasty* was soon to become a big ratings smash. But on the football field, those two words were no longer synonymous. The Cowboys would remain competitive in the post-Staubach era, but they would not return to the Super Bowl until the 1990s.

Breaking through the arms of Alonzo Jackson, Tony Dorsett scores his second touchdown of the game. This contest was held on October 20, 1986.

SUPER MEN ONCE AGAIN

3

On March 31, 1980, the greatest Cowboy legend of all rode off into the sunset: Roger Staubach officially announced his retirement. Quarterback Danny White would take over the reins of the Dallas offense. A backup to Staubach for four seasons, White knew Tom Landry's system as well as anyone. The Cowboys still boasted many of their Pro Bowl stars from the 1970s, including running back Tony Dorsett, tight end Billy Joe Dupree, and wide receiver Drew Pearson.

An efficient passer, White led the 'Boys to a 12–4 record in 1980. They steamrolled the Rams in the playoffs, 34–13, then came from behind to knock off Atlanta. In that game, White threw 2 touchdown passes to Pearson—the second with less than a minute to go—to prevail 30–27. The Cowboys traveled to play Philadelphia in the NFC Championship Game. It was bitterly cold, with a wind chill of −16°F. It was so frigid, in fact, that Landry traded his trademark fedora for a fur Cossack hat. The Eagles proceeded to ice the Cowboys 20–7.

In 1981, Dallas went 12–4 again to claim the NFC Eastern Division title. Dorsett enjoyed the greatest year of his career, rushing for 1,646 yards. In the first playoff game, the Cowboys crushed the Tampa Bay Buccaneers 38–0. Though they made the NFC Championship Game for the ninth time in twelve years, the Cowboys lost a heartbreaker to San Francisco. With a minute remaining, the 49ers' Joe Montana fired one of the most famous passes in football history. Dwight Clark leaped high in the back of the end zone for "The Catch," giving San Francisco a 28–27 victory.

⊖Expectations Deflated

A players' strike washed out nearly half of the 1982 season. However, with a 6–3 record, Dallas made the playoffs for the sixteenth time in seventeen years. White, Dorsett, and wide receiver Tony Hill continued to power the potent Cowboys offense. Dallas dismantled Tampa Bay (30–17) and Green Bay (37–26) in the playoffs, advancing once again to the NFC Championship Game. Quarterback Gary Hogeboom started in place of an injured White, and Dallas lost to Washington 31–17. The Cowboys, it appeared, did not have a

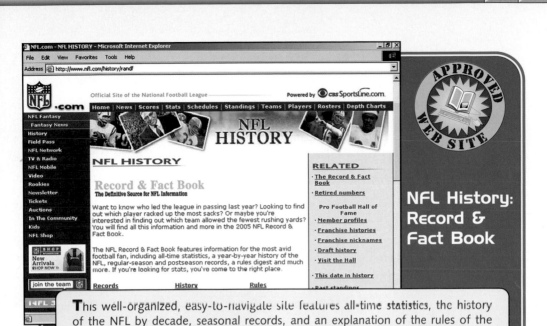

This well-organized, easy-to-navigate site features all-time statistics, the history of the NFL by decade, seasonal records, and an explanation of the rules of the game. Find out information on individual, team, and defensive records.

EDITOR'S CHOICE

Access this Web site from http://www.myreportlinks.com

QB who could win the big game. *If only Roger Staubach was still around,* so many fans muttered.

White kept plugging away. In 1983, he smashed team records for yards passing (3,980) and touchdown tosses (29). The Cowboys posted another 12–4 record, and set an NFL mark with their ninth straight playoff appearance. The day after Christmas, fans expected Dallas to cruise past the Rams in the opening playoff game. Instead, Los Angeles pulled off a 24–17 upset at Texas Stadium. The Cowboys not only lost this postseason game, but they also would not win any for the rest of the decade.

→ Bum's Bums

In 1984, the Murchison family sold the Cowboys to a group headed by Dallas area businessman H. R. "Bum" Bright. They paid $63 million for the team and $20 million for Texas Stadium, which would prove to be incredible bargains. White and Hogeboom shared quarterback duties in 1984, but neither could muster any magic. The Cowboys scored 308 points and gave up 308—and they did not make the playoffs.

The Cowboys remodeled Texas Stadium in 1985. They installed DiamondVision color scoreboards, and they added more private suites than any other NFL team. Coach Landry's club sneaked into the postseason in 1985 thanks largely to 33 interceptions. The defensive backfield, led by Dennis Thurman, was nicknamed "Thurman's Thieves." However, Dallas was shut out by the Rams 20–0 in the first playoff game. This was the start of a half decade of misery for Cowboys fans.

In 1986, Bright wanted a more exciting offense. He hired a young coach, Paul Hackett, to be the offensive mastermind. During the season, though, Hackett clashed with "old school" head coach Tom Landry. The offense was a disaster. Dorsett struggled to run because of sore knees. Quarterback Steve Pelluer was sacked 11 times in one game. Dallas went 1–7 in the second half of the season to finish 7–9. It ended a streak of twenty consecutive winning seasons, the longest in NFL history.

➲ Bum Times for the 'Boys

The 1987 season was an even bigger fiasco. NFL players went on strike again, and teams played several games with replacement players. Tex Schramm had worded the contracts of his star players so that they had to play—or else lose tremendous amounts of money. Thus, White, Dorsett, and others "crossed the picket line" and suited up. This angered striking players on the team and throughout the NFL. Said the Cowboys' Everson Walls, "People used to hate us out of respect. Now they hate us out of disrespect."[1] Once again, the Cowboys finished 7–9.

In 1988, Landry tied a league record by coaching in his twenty-ninth consecutive season with the same team. Yet it was the worst of his career. The Cowboys fielded too many inexperienced players who made too many mistakes. In a seven-game stretch, Dallas lost five games in the final minute. Powerful Herschel Walker, who rushed for 1,514 yards, was the lone bright spot. The team finished 3–13—the worst record in the NFL. Landry was criticized for being confused during critical moments of games. Bright wanted him fired, but the owner had bigger problems. His

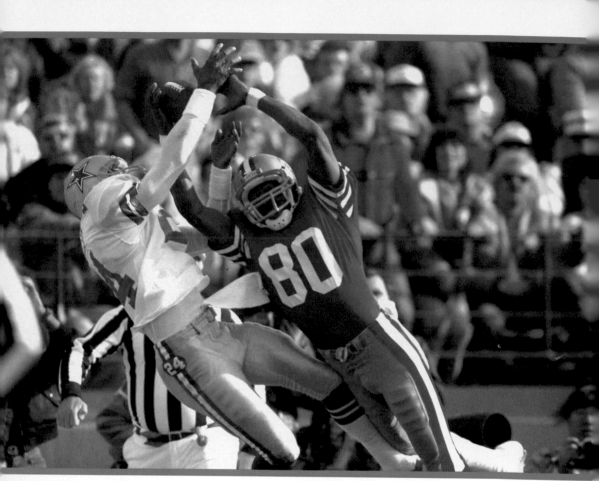

▲ In a fight for the ball, Cowboys cornerback Everson Walls breaks up what could have been a catch for 49ers receiver Jerry Rice.

personal fortune was dwindling, so much so that he needed to sell the team.

⊖The Fateful Dinner

In February 1989, oilman Jerry Jones bought the Cowboys for $140 million. Days later, Jones dined at Landry's favorite restaurant, Mia's, with University of Miami head coach Jimmy Johnson.

Jones and Johnson had been football teammates at the University of Arkansas. When a photo of Jones and Johnson appeared in the next day's newspaper, everyone realized the inevitable: Landry would be fired and Johnson would become the new head coach.

Three days later, Landry met with his players to say good-bye. The old coach cried, and his players gave him a standing ovation. Fans responded with an outpouring of love. They stuck "Landry for Governor" bumper stickers on their cars and pickups, and fifty thousand fans attended a Tom Landry Day parade on April 22. Even President George H. W. Bush sent a telegram of support.

Jones was despised in the Cowboys offices, and not just because he axed coach Landry. Jones fired many employees, including Gil Brandt—the team's director of scouting for close to thirty years. Tex Schramm resigned. Jerry Jones and Jimmy Johnson would run the Cowboys.

The Joke of the League

The first season under coach Johnson, 1989, was catastrophic. The team finished 1–15. Years of poor drafting had left the team painfully short on talent. Rookie quarterback Troy Aikman showed great promise, but his porous offensive line left him vulnerable. The Cowboys became the laughingstock of pro football. Even Dallas fans were cracking jokes such as this one: "A guy discovers that his car has been broken into, and he thinks, 'I hope they didn't take my Cowboy season tickets.' When he checks the car, he finds that the thief has left an extra set of tickets."[2]

Who's Laughing Now?

The best thing that happened during the 1989 season was when the Cowboys traded Herschel Walker to Minnesota for five players and six high draft picks. In 1990, Dallas selected running back Emmitt Smith. The rookie ran for 937 yards that fall and looked like a future superstar. The Cowboys improved to 7–9.

The 1991 NFL Draft turned into a bonanza for the Cowboys. They landed numerous future starters, headed by defensive tackle Russell Maryland. In the fifth game of the season, against the New York Giants, the Cowboys came alive. Smith rushed for 182 yards. Aikman completed 20 of 27 passes. And Michael Irvin, a phenomenal young receiver known as "The Playmaker," caught 6 passes for 91 yards. This trio, it appeared, could lead Dallas back to prominence.

After defeating the powerful Redskins, Smith exclaimed, "We shocked the world!"[3] Dallas finished the season at 11–5, and Smith led the NFL in rushing with 1,563 yards. In the playoffs, the Cowboys upset Chicago before losing to Detroit.

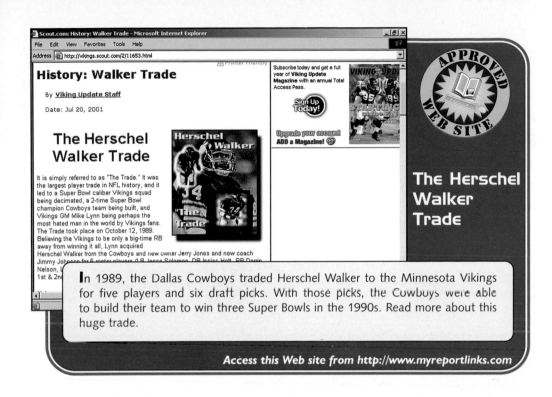

Scout.com: History: Walker Trade - Microsoft Internet Explorer

File   Edit   View   Favorites   Tools   Help

Address   http://vikings.scout.com/2/11653.html

History: Walker Trade

By **Viking Update Staff**

Date: Jul 20, 2001

The Herschel Walker Trade

It is simply referred to as "The Trade." It was the largest player trade in NFL history, and it led to a Super Bowl caliber Vikings squad being decimated, a 2-time Super Bowl champion Cowboys team being built, and Vikings GM Mike Lynn being perhaps the most hated man in the world by Vikings fans. The Trade took place on October 12, 1989. Believing the Vikings to be only a big-time RB away from winning it all, Lynn acquired Herschel Walker from the Cowboys and new owner Jerry Jones and new coach Jimmy Johnson for 5 roster players (LB Jesse Solomon, DB Issiac Holt, RB Darrin Nelson, 1st & 2nd

Subscribe today and get a full year of **Viking Update** Magazine with an annual Total Access Pass.

Sign Up Today!

Upgrade your account **ADD a Magazine!** GO!

The Herschel Walker Trade

In 1989, the Dallas Cowboys traded Herschel Walker to the Minnesota Vikings for five players and six draft picks. With those picks, the Cowboys were able to build their team to win three Super Bowls in the 1990s. Read more about this huge trade.

Access this Web site from http://www.myreportlinks.com

Fans of the 'Boys could not wait for the next season to kick off.

⊝ Super Bowl Blowout

In 1992, the Cowboys reemerged as America's Team. They not only sold out all their home games, but they also set an NFL record for highest road attendance. Nate Newton, Mark Stepnoski, and tight end Jay Novacek anchored an improved offensive line. Aikman, Irvin, and Smith joined those players as Pro Bowl selections. Smith again paced the league in rushing (1,713 yards), and the defense allowed the fewest yards in the NFL. Dallas finished with a team-record thirteen wins.

In the playoffs, the Cowboys ran wild over Philadelphia (34–10) and San Francisco (30–20). In Pasadena, California, 98,374 fans arrived to see the Cowboys take on Buffalo in Super Bowl XXVII. The Bills were appearing in their third straight Super Bowl. With 133.4 million television viewers, this became the most watched event in TV history.

The Bills took a 7–0 lead, but then the Cowboys struck like lightning. First, Aikman fired a 23-yard touchdown pass to Novacek. Then, moments later, Dallas defensive tackle Jimmie

The Official Web Site of Troy Aikman offers an insiders view of the Hall of Fame quarterback. Learn about Aikman's high school, college, and professional football days while viewing video footage and photos.

Jones scooped up a fumble and ran it in for a touchdown. Aikman hit Michael Irvin for 2 touchdown passes in the second quarter to give the Cowboys a 28–10 halftime lead.

The explosive Dallas offense, combined with a defense that forced 9 turnovers, produced a 52–17 blowout. Late in the game, 292-pound Cowboy Leon Lett picked up a fumble and rumbled 64 yards. Had he not celebrated before reaching the goal line (which led to his own fumble), Dallas would have scored 58 or 59 points. Still, the Cowboys were ecstatic. Beamed Nate Newton, "I am so filled with joy, I can't even express it. If I could explode, I would."[4]

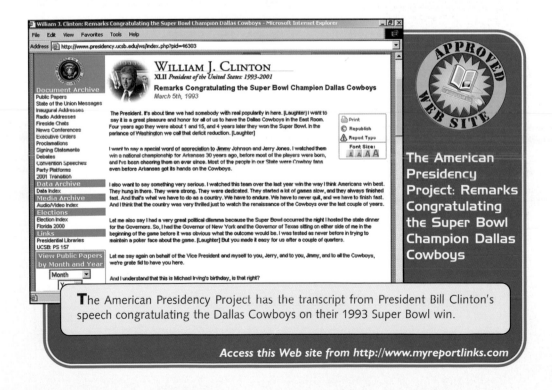

The American Presidency Project: Remarks Congratulating the Super Bowl Champion Dallas Cowboys

The American Presidency Project has the transcript from President Bill Clinton's speech congratulating the Dallas Cowboys on their 1993 Super Bowl win.

Access this Web site from http://www.myreportlinks.com

➔'Boys vs. Bills——The Rematch

In March 1993, the Cowboys visited the White House and shook hands with President Bill Clinton. Come fall, they began to make *Sports Illustrated*'s prediction that they would repeat as champs a reality. With an overtime win against the New York Giants, Dallas finished the season at 12–4. The team sent an NFC-record eleven players to the Pro Bowl, including seven offensive starters. Emmitt Smith won his third NFL rushing crown, with 1,486 yards. After dispatching Green Bay and San Francisco in the playoffs,

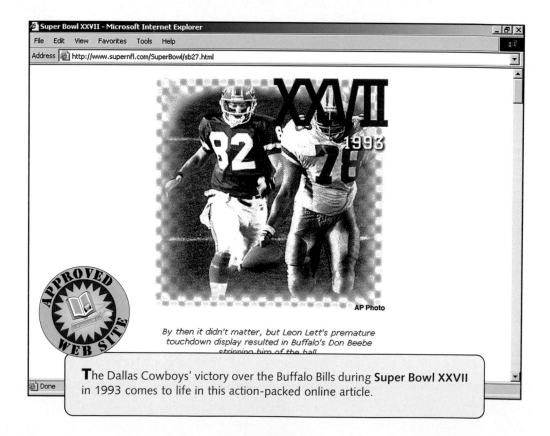

AP Photo

By then it didn't matter, but Leon Lett's premature touchdown display resulted in Buffalo's Don Beebe stripping him of the ball.

The Dallas Cowboys' victory over the Buffalo Bills during **Super Bowl XXVII** in 1993 comes to life in this action-packed online article.

the 'Boys returned to the Super Bowl for a record seventh time.

The Bills, having lost three straight Super Bowls, garnered everyone's sympathy—except the Cowboys.' Buffalo lcd 13–6 at halftime, but Dallas outscored the Bills 24–0 over the last thirty minutes. Cowboys safety James Washington returned a fumble 46 yards for a touchdown, and Emmitt Smith rushed for 2 TDs of his own.

Smith earned game MVP honors, but much of the credit went to the Cowboys' enormous offensive line. Nate Newton said the Bills wore down because they were "messing with a bunch of 350-pound men."[5] With the victory, the Cowboys tied Pittsburgh for the most Super Bowl titles with four.

➲ New Coach, Another Title

Coach Jimmy Johnson had found the 1993 season especially stressful. After owner Jerry Jones boasted that 'any one of five hundred coaches could have won the Super Bowl' with all the talent that Jones had acquired, Johnson resigned. Jones replaced him with another one of his connections from Arkansas. Barry Switzer had been an assistant coach for the 1964 Razorbacks national championship team. The legendary University of Oklahoma coach had no NFL experience. He also had a reputation for running a "loose ship." But like Jones said, anybody could win with this kind of talent.

On August 15, 1994, the Cowboys played the Houston Oilers in a preseason game in Mexico City in front of an NFL-record 112,376 fans. Throughout the season, Dallas packed stadiums around the league. The Cowboys went 12–4 again while sending another eleven players to the Pro Bowl. For the second straight year, the entire backfield went Pro Bowling in Hawaii, including fullback Daryl "Moose" Johnston.

The Cowboys crushed the Packers in the play-offs 35–9, but they lost to San Francisco in the NFC Championship Game 38–28. The dream of winning three straight Super Bowls—an unprecedented feat—was over. Few criticized the Cowboys, since the 49ers were an outstanding team (13–3). "My hat is off to them," said Jerry Jones. "They're the champions. They're going to the Super Bowl. But I would not trade their team straight up for my team, at all."[6]

⊖ Switzer Delivers

Good thing he did not. In 1995, San Francisco went 11–5 and lost its first playoff game. The Cowboys, meanwhile, finished 12–4. They blew out Philadelphia 30–11, and knocked off Green Bay 38–27, in the NFC Championship Game. Dallas had weathered a tumultuous season (see

▲ While playing for the Cowboys in the 1990s, Daryl "Moose" Johnston was considered one of the best fullbacks in the league. Here he is shown barreling over Corey Raymond of the New York Giants.

Chapter 1). But with their 27–17 triumph over Pittsburgh, they became the first team to win three Super Bowls in four years.

Tom Landry and Tex Schramm were distant memories. So, too, was the 1–15 season of 1989. The Cowboys had endured the jokes to become one of the mightiest teams in football history.

▲ *"The Playmaker," Michael Irvin, celebrates after a touchdown reception against the Kansas City Chiefs during the 1995 season.*

UPS AND DOWNS

4

In the late 1980s, the Cowboys did not have enough stars. In 1996, they had too many.

Because of the NFL's salary cap, each team could spend only a limited amount of money on players' salaries. Dallas had a large number of players eligible to leave the team as free agents in 1996. Since the Cowboys could not pay everyone what they wanted, some of those players were destined to leave. The coaches braced themselves for a tougher season in 1996. What they did not expect was losing Michael Irvin.

The flamboyant receiver loved to have a good time. Unfortunately, he sometimes overdid it. On March 4, 1996, while celebrating his thirtieth birthday, Irvin was arrested for drug use. He was sentenced to four years probation, and the NFL suspended him for the first five games of the 1996 season. Clearly, the Cowboys were not the same without "The Playmaker." They opened the season at 1–3.

While the Dallas offense ranked twenty-fifth in the NFL, the defense remained tough. The Cowboys finished 10–6 to secure their eighteenth division title. Dallas routed Minnesota in the NFC Wildcard Game 40–15, but it lost the next week to Carolina 26–17.

The Cowboys opened their 1997 season at 6–5. If they could win their next game at Green Bay, they felt they could make the playoffs. But after a 10–10 first half at frigid Lambeau Field, the Packers outscored Dallas 35–7 in the final thirty minutes. "I can't remember a loss like this," said Emmitt Smith.[1] Indeed, it was the Cowboys' worst defeat of the decade. They went on to lose their last five games to finish 6–10. After the season, head coach Barry Switzer resigned.

Gailey and "The Triplets"

In February 1998, Cowboys owner Jerry Jones hired Chan Gailey as the fourth head coach in team history. Gailey, who had been the Pittsburgh Steelers offensive coordinator, helped rejuvenate the Cowboys offense. In their first twelve games in 1998, they scored at least thirty points seven times. In one game, Emmitt Smith set the NFL career record for rushing touchdowns. In another, Deion

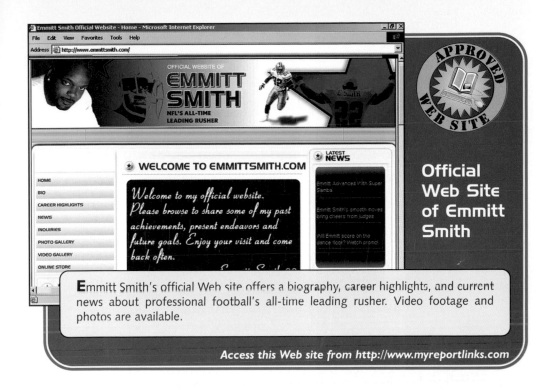

Emmitt Smith's official Web site offers a biography, career highlights, and current news about professional football's all-time leading rusher. Video footage and photos are available.

Access this Web site from http://www.myreportlinks.com

Sanders returned a punt *and* an interception for TDs. Dallas ran roughshod over its division rivals, going 8–0 against the NFC East. The Cowboys finished 10–6, but they lost to Arizona in the NFC Wildcard Game.

For eight straight years, Aikman, Smith, and Irvin had been the team's passing, rushing, and receiving leaders. But the reign of "The Triplets" drew to a close in 1999. Aikman missed two games due to a concussion, one of ten that he suffered in his career. It was clear that he was close to retirement. Smith made the Pro Bowl for the eighth time—and his last. On October 10, Irvin was forced to retire after suffering a serious injury.

In the 1999 season opener, however, each of "The Triplets" starred in an amazing comeback against the Washington Redskins. Trailing 35–14, Smith scored with 10:43 remaining in the game. With 2 touchdown passes from Aikman to Irvin, Dallas miraculously tied the score 35–35. In overtime, Aikman hit Raghib "Rocket" Ismail for a 76-yard touchdown. Aikman went on to win eight games in 1999, making him the first quarterback in NFL history to win ninety in a decade. Though they finished at 8–8, the Cowboys somehow made the playoffs. Their exit was predictably quick, as Minnesota beat them 27–10 in the opening playoff game.

⊜A Tip of the Fedora for Landry

After the 1999 season, the news in Dallas was all about coaches. Jones fired Gailey and replaced him with Cowboys defensive coordinator Dave Campo. Then, on February 12, 2000, Cowboys coaching legend Tom Landry died of leukemia. All across Texas and beyond, fans praised Landry as a man of great character. Old friend Kathryn Johnson remembered how Landry treated his kids when they were little. "Tom would always, right before the children's bedtime, have devotionals, read the Bible, and discuss it with them," Johnson said. "Then he'd carry them to bed. That meant so much to my children, to get to see that."[2]

This fun-filled Web site offers basic information about the positions on a football team and how to play them. Facts about football, up-to-date league standings, and statistics are also included.

Access this Web site from http://www.myreportlinks.com

During the 2000 season, the Cowboys honored Landry by wearing fedora emblems on their sleeves. However, fans had little to get excited about. Aikman suffered another concussion in the season opener, and injuries decimated the team. After losing 31–0 in the season finale, Dallas finished 5–11.

Whatever direction the Cowboys were headed, they would have to go without Troy Aikman. Due to concerns about his health, Dallas waived the twelve-year veteran in March 2001. A month later, he retired. "You watch and you think that your time will never come," Aikman said as he fought back tears. "And my time's come."[3]

→ Bad Records, New Record

Entering 2001, the Cowboys were rated by *Sports Illustrated* as the worst team in the NFL. Bad drafts and lack of discipline had ruined the team. As an example, cornerback Kareem Larrimore was fined eleven times for breaking team rules in 2000 and 2001. Yet the Cowboys still kept him on the roster.

Dallas finished 5–11 again in 2001. Offensive lineman Larry Allen was the only player to make the Pro Bowl. Coach Campo employed four quarterbacks in the absence of Aikman: Quincy Carter, Ryan Leaf, Clint Stoerner, and Anthony Wright. Not one of them threw more than five touchdown passes all season, as the Cowboys finished thirtieth in the NFL in scoring.

As fans watched in dismay, the Cowboys finished 5–11 for the third straight year in 2002. Quarterbacks Carter and Chad Hutchinson led an offense that averaged less than 14 points per game. On October 27, however, Dallas fans had something to cheer about. At Texas Stadium, Emmitt Smith blasted up the middle for 11 yards. With the historic run, he eclipsed Walter Payton's NFL rushing record of 16,726 yards.

The Cowboys celebrated Texas-style after the game, complete with flags, balloons, and fireworks. Smith ran a "victory lap" around the field, hugging dozens of people. He saved his longest

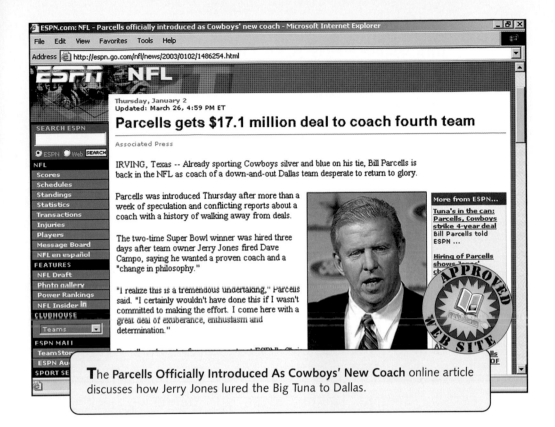

ESPN.com: NFL - Parcells officially introduced as Cowboys' new coach - Microsoft Internet Explorer

File   Edit   View   Favorites   Tools   Help

Address http://espn.go.com/nfl/news/2003/0102/1486254.html

ESPN NFL

Thursday, January 2
Updated: March 26, 4:59 PM ET

Parcells gets $17.1 million deal to coach fourth team

Associated Press

IRVING, Texas -- Already sporting Cowboys silver and blue on his tie, Bill Parcells is back in the NFL as coach of a down-and-out Dallas team desperate to return to glory.

Parcells was introduced Thursday after more than a week of speculation and conflicting reports about a coach with a history of walking away from deals.

The two-time Super Bowl winner was hired three days after team owner Jerry Jones fired Dave Campo, saying he wanted a proven coach and a "change in philosophy."

"I realize this is a tremendous undertaking," Parcells said. "I certainly wouldn't have done this if I wasn't committed to making the effort. I come here with a great deal of exuberance, enthusiasm and determination."

More from ESPN...

Tuna's in the can:
Parcells, Cowboys
strike 4-year deal
Bill Parcells told
ESPN ...

Hiring of Parcells
shows ...

The **Parcells Officially Introduced As Cowboys' New Coach** online article discusses how Jerry Jones lured the Big Tuna to Dallas.

embrace for Daryl Johnston, the fullback who had blocked for him for ten years.

The "Big Tuna"

By February 2003, many Dallas fans were ashamed of their team. That month, four current or former Cowboys were in the news because of crimes they had allegedly committed. This team needed help. It needed the "Big Tuna."

Jerry Jones made his smartest move of the new millennium when he hired Bill Parcells as head coach. The Big Tuna was considered the best coach in the NFL. He had transformed the New York Giants and New England Patriots from bottom feeders to Super Bowl teams. Parcells worked from early morning to late at night, and he demanded total effort. "Even if you're the most veteran player, some time in training camp you've got to prove to me you can play," he said. "I can't go on 'might do.' Nobody gets a free pass. They have to prove it."[4]

⊜ Some Improvement

Stunningly, Parcells whipped the Cowboys into a playoff contender. The defense, which was mediocre in 2002, allowed the fewest yards in the NFL in 2003. Linebacker Dexter Coakley, defensive lineman La'Roi Glover, and defensive back Roy Williams all made the Pro Bowl. Quincy Carter started every game at quarterback, and Troy Hambrick rushed for 972 yards.

Dallas finished 10–6 in the 2003 season and made the playoffs. Unfortunately for the Cowboys, their opponent in the NFC Wildcard Game brought its "A" game. The Carolina Panthers did not commit a single penalty or turnover en route to a 29–10 victory.

In 2004, Parcells gave his old quarterback with the New York Jets, Vinny Testaverde, a chance to lead the Cowboys. Testaverde had thrown for more than 40,000 yards in his career. However, he

▲ Cowboys safety Roy Williams flips Vikings receiver Marcus Robinson. Williams was selected to play in the 2003 Pro Bowl.

was forty years old. For Dallas in 2004, he completed 60 percent of his passes but led the NFL with 20 interceptions. Turnovers and penalties frustrated Parcells, and the defense regressed significantly. The Cowboys slumped to 6–10.

For 2005, Parcells turned to another of his former quarterbacks. The Cowboys acquired Drew Bledsoe, who had led New England to the Super Bowl in January 1997. Parcells also stressed a return to fundamentals, demanding that his players minimize penalties and turnovers.

Bledsoe rejuvenated the Cowboys offense, throwing for 3,639 yards and 23 touchdowns. Terry Glenn, another former Patriot, was Bledsoe's favorite target (1,136 yards receiving). Running

NFL Players.com: Cowboys

All of the current Dallas Cowboys are listed on this Web site. Click on a specific name to find out the individual's number, read his biography, and view his statistics. Some entries feature an interview with the player and/or journal entries.

Access this Web site from http://www.myreportlinks.com

back Julius Jones rushed for 993 yards. Entering the final Sunday of the season, the Cowboys were 9–6 and had a chance to make the playoffs. However, Dallas was eliminated when Carolina and Washington won early in the day. Emotionally deflated, Dallas lost its game to lowly St. Louis 20–10.

⇒ Future Drama

Certainly, Jerry Jones had made a sound decision by hiring Parcells. Yet the maverick team owner still flirted with controversy. On March 18, 2006, the Cowboys signed the most talked about player in the NFL: Terrell Owens. A game-breaking, superstar receiver, Owens had also made numerous enemies in recent seasons. With San Francisco and Philadelphia, he had bad-mouthed his quarterbacks and haggled with team owners about his contracts.

The national media predicted a soap opera in Dallas, starring Parcells and Owens. While the coach kept his cool, Owens continued to showboat. After a touchdown against Washington, he lay in the end zone and used the football as a pillow. More alarmingly, he overdosed on pain medication on September 27 and was rushed to the hospital. Parcells found solace in new starting quarterback Tony Romo, who seemed capable of bringing the Cowboys back to greatness. After a playoff loss, the Big Tuna resigned in January 2007.

Tom Landry waves to the Texas Stadium crowd after being inducted into the Cowboys Ring of Honor.

THE MASTERMINDS

5

The Cowboys have been around for close to a half century. Yet for most of that time, the team was run by three men: head coach Tom Landry, general manager Tex Schramm, and personnel director Gil Brandt. This section profiles the trio that built "America's Team"—as well as four modern mavericks who pumped new life into the franchise.

Tom Landry

They do not usually name schools after football coaches, but they did in Irving, Texas. At Tom Landry Elementary School, L-A-N-D-R-Y stands for Loyal, Achieving, Neighborly, Disciplined, Ready, and You are a leader. These traits also describe the legendary coach.

Born on September 11, 1924, Landry flew thirty bombing missions during World War II. He even survived a crash in Belgium. After playing in the NFL and serving as an assistant coach, he was named the Cowboys' first head coach in 1960. He remained in the position for twenty-nine seasons.

While other coaches dressed casually on the sidelines, Landry always wore a suit and a fedora hat. He virtually never displayed emotion, which his players found comforting. He explained: "Leadership is a matter of having people look at you and gain confidence. If you're in control, they're in control."[1]

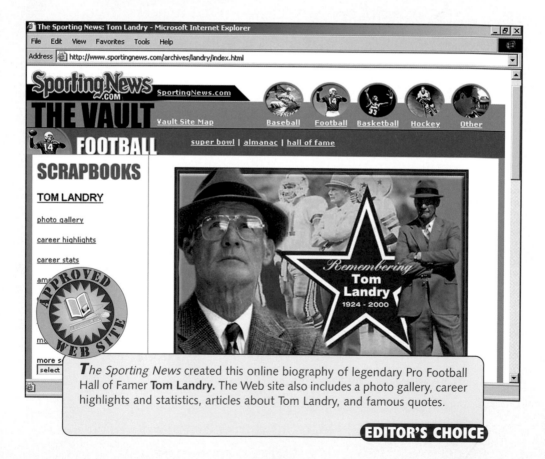

The Sporting News created this online biography of legendary Pro Football Hall of Famer **Tom Landry.** The Web site also includes a photo gallery, career highlights and statistics, articles about Tom Landry, and famous quotes.

EDITOR'S CHOICE

Despite his conservative appearance, Landry was one of the game's greatest innovators. He utilized the "shotgun formation," in which the quarterback lined up several steps behind the center. His "flex defense" allowed his linemen to react more quickly against the opposing offense.

Landry won 270 games in his career, third most in NFL history. He captured thirteen division titles and went to five Super Bowls, winning two. His 20 consecutive winning seasons remains an NFL record.

Tex Schramm

Football historians credit Tex Schramm for making the Cowboys "America's Team." But he also helped make football America's game.

The twelfth child of his California parents, Schramm was named Texas because, he said, his parents ran out of names. Though he worked in the Los Angeles Rams front office for more than a decade, Tex was destined for the Lone Star State. In 1959, he became the Cowboys' first general manager.

Schramm's innovations were endless. He utilized computer technology to improve the Cowboys' scouting system. He also infused excitement into the game. He premiered the Dallas Cowboys Cheerleaders, and he brought Cowboys games to Thanksgiving Day. Schramm also pulled off spectacular Draft Day trades. Bob Lilly, Ed "Too Tall" Jones, and Randy White were all last-minute acquisitions.

At the league level, Schramm wielded about as much power as the commissioner. He helped coordinate the merger of the NFL and AFL in 1966, and he spearheaded the following innovations:

- a microphone for the head referee during penalty announcements
- moving the hash marks closer to the middle of the field to spur more offense
- sudden-death overtime
- a six-division, wild-card playoff system
- instant replay

Schramm served the Cowboys for twenty-nine seasons, resigning right after Landry was fired. "The National Football League continues to prosper from Tex's insight and innovation," said team owner Jerry Jones. "His fingerprints are all over today's game."[2]

⊖Gil Brandt

No one knew it at the time, but Cowboys owner Clint Murchison made shrewd decisions around 1960. He hired Tex Schramm as general manager and Tom Landry as head coach. He also okayed Schramm's recommendation to hire Gil Brandt as the Cowboys' chief talent scout. Like Schramm and Landry, Brandt became one of the very best at his craft.

From 1960 to 1989, Brandt signed or traded for forty-eight Pro Bowl players for the Cowboys. He drafted twenty-seven future Pro Bowlers—nearly one per season. The feat is especially impressive because the Cowboys, as a perennially winning team, usually drafted low in each round. Moreover, Brandt earned praise around the NFL for his ability to discover talented players at small schools. For example, he drafted safety Cliff Harris out of tiny Ouachita Baptist. Harris went on to become a six-time Pro Bowl selection.

Jerry Jones dismissed Brandt in 1989 shortly after firing Landry. In 2006, Brandt remained active, serving as a senior analyst for NFL.com.

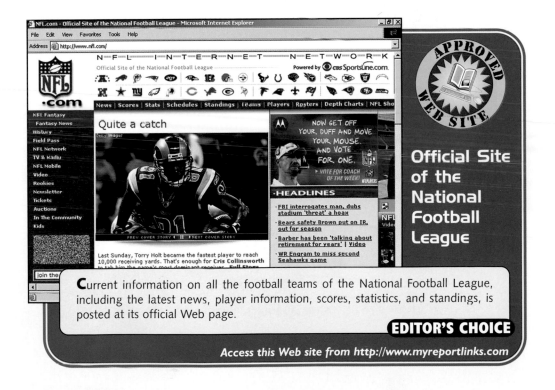

Current information on all the football teams of the National Football League, including the latest news, player information, scores, statistics, and standings, is posted at its official Web page.

EDITOR'S CHOICE

Access this Web site from http://www.myreportlinks.com

Jerry Jones

In 1964, Jerry Jones and Jimmy Johnson were teammates on a University of Arkansas team which won the national championship. Little did they know that three decades later they would lead the Dallas Cowboys to a pair of Super Bowl titles.

In his early days in the corporate world, Jones endured several failed business ventures. But, he frequently points out, "I am a risk-taker."[3] And many of his risks were hugely successful. In the 1970s and 1980s, he became fabulously wealthy in the oil business. In 1989, he took another gamble—buying the 3–13 Cowboys for $140 million. Jones was so brazen that he fired head coach Tom Landry. In the minds of Texans, it was like telling Abraham Lincoln to hit the road.

In the NFL, two things hardly ever work: an owner who meddles in day-to-day operations, and a college coach who jumps straight to the NFL. But that was how things were done in Dallas. Jones served as general manager, and Johnson took over as head coach. With Jones cheering on the sidelines at every game, the Cowboys won Super Bowls in 1992–93 and 1993–94.

Jones was on a roll. In 1995–96, he won his third Super Bowl with another former college coach: Barry Switzer. Jones's $140 million gamble

▲ Jerry Jones (left) and Jimmy Johnson (right) celebrate the Cowboys' victory over the Buffalo Bills in Super Bowl XXVII. Emmitt Smith is standing behind them.

paid off big time. By the 2000s, his team was valued at more than $900 million.

⊜Jimmy Johnson

About the only thing that looked good on the 1–15 Cowboys in 1989 was Jimmy Johnson's hair. The head coach starched it into a fashionable wave. They called it "helmet hair" because of its hard, shiny texture. But beneath his fancy "do" was a brilliant mind. On an IQ test in his younger days, Johnson had scored 162—about the equivalent of Albert Einstein.

Prior to joining Dallas in 1989, Johnson had posted a 52–9 record at the University of Miami. The rookie NFL coach understood the Cowboys' shortcomings. The team was too old and too slow. Over the next several seasons, Johnson and the Cowboys acquired phenomenally talented players through the draft and free agency.

In 1990, Dallas improved to 7–9—then jumped to 11–5 in 1991. Johnson was exceptionally skilled at judging defensive talent. As a result, the Cowboys led the NFL in fewest yards allowed in 1992. Johnson won the Super Bowl that year as well as the following season, becoming only the fourth coach in NFL history to win back-to-back Super Bowls.

Johnson will never forget the second title. President Bill Clinton phoned him in the locker

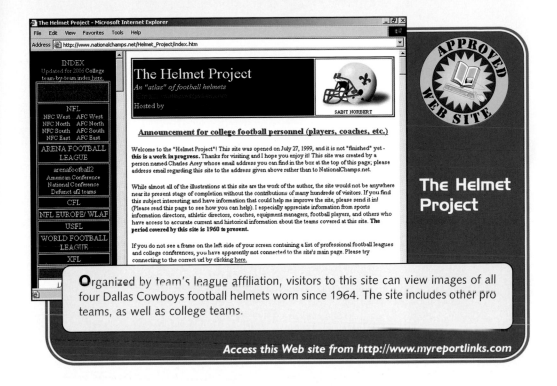

The Helmet Project
An "atlas" of football helmets

The Helmet Project

Organized by team's league affiliation, visitors to this site can view images of all four Dallas Cowboys football helmets worn since 1964. The site includes other pro teams, as well as college teams.

Access this Web site from http://www.myreportlinks.com

room, and running back Emmitt Smith poured Gatorade on his head. For once, fans got to see Coach Johnson with his hair down.

⊝ Barry Switzer

After his days at Arkansas, Barry Switzer became a coaching legend at the University of Oklahoma. With his famed Wishbone offense, he led the Sooners to a record of 157–29–2 in the 1970s and 1980s. His .837 winning percentage ranks among the best in NCAA history, and he won three national championships.

After Johnson left the Cowboys in early 1994, Jones shocked the sports world by hiring Switzer as head coach. Switzer had not coached in five years, and he had never played or coached in the NFL. Moreover, his 1980s Oklahoma teams had been accused of lacking discipline. Somehow, Switzer kept the Cowboys dynasty alive. He went 12–4 in both 1994 and 1995, winning the Super Bowl the latter season.

Switzer retired two years later with a career NFL regular season record of 40–24. Like Jimmy Johnson, he had made Jones look like a genius.

Bill Parcells

In 2003, after three straight 5–11 seasons, the Cowboys needed a hard-driving coach to pull them out of their rut. They found him in Bill Parcells.

The Big Tuna had a history of turning losing teams into champions. He transformed the New York Giants (3–12–1 in 1983) into Super Bowl victors in 1986 and 1990. He guided New England (2–14 in 1992) to the Super Bowl in 1996. And he sparked the New York Jets (1–15 in 1996) to the AFC Championship Game two years later.

In 2003, his first year in Dallas, Parcells doubled the Cowboys' win total to ten. Moreover, he became the first NFL head coach ever to guide four different teams to the playoffs. Cowboys owner Jerry Jones praised him for bringing "enthusiasm and determination" to town.[4]

▲ Bill Parcells gives a little tough love to one of his players during a 2003 game.

Parcells has also used frequent tongue-lashings to motivate his players. "If you're sensitive, you will have a hard time with me," he said. "The only players I hurt with my words are the ones who have an inflated opinion of their ability. I can't worry about that."[5]

Dallas players knew not to question Parcells, who made the NFL's All-Decade Team as the league's best coach of the 1990s. Like the Cowboys' first team leader, Tom Landry, the Big Tuna is destined for the Pro Football Hall of Fame.

▲ Cowboys fans almost always pack Texas Stadium to root for their team.

WELCOME TO TEXAS STADIUM

6

Why does Texas Stadium have a big "hole" in its roof? "So that God can watch His team," explained former Cowboy D. D. Lewis.[1] Many folks in Texas, where football is practically religion, nod in agreement.

The reason for the opening has more to do with money and engineering rather than religion. Back in the late 1960s, the Cowboys wanted to move out of the antiquated Cotton Bowl and build a state-of-the-art stadium. They broke ground in Irving, a suburb just west of Dallas. Originally, it was supposed to be a domed stadium. But engineers realized that the structure was not strong enough to support a complete roof. Planners discussed adding more structural support, but funds to do so were not available.

Thus, the Cowboys were left with a partial roof that covered most of the seats. The rest of the playing field was left vulnerable to rain and snow. Many season ticket holders think it is a win-win situation: They can watch true outdoor football without getting soaked themselves. The roof also protects fans from the scorching sun on hot September afternoons.

Ins and Outs of Texas Stadium

Texas Stadium cost $35 million to build, and it opened on October 24, 1971. Initially, the venue was as holy as it was "holey:" Its first event was a crusade by evangelist Billy Graham. Soon, fans packed the stadium for football.

Texas Stadium seats 65,675 fans, many of whom watch in luxury. In fact, the stadium boasts 381 luxury suites, more than any sports stadium in the country. The suites circle the entire stadium at two levels. Midlevel suites sell for about $500,000 each, while those in the upper level fetch roughly $2 million apiece. Typically, large companies own the suites, using them as perks for their employees and clients.

As newcomers enter the seating area, they immediately notice several features. First, of course, is the roof, with a hole that measures 2.5 acres. In addition, two large DiamondVision video screens provide information, entertainment, and replays. Above, five Super Bowl banners hang from the rafters. Below, a soft artificial surface

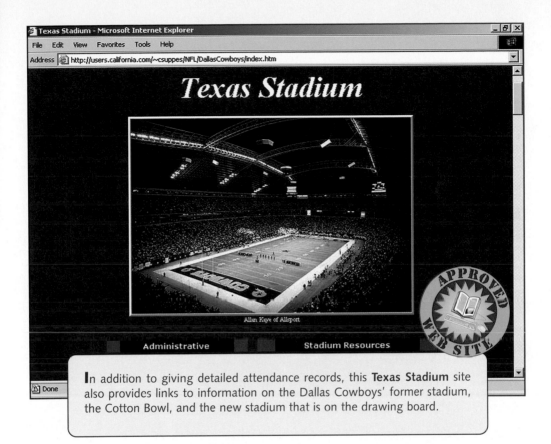

Texas Stadium - Microsoft Internet Explorer

File   Edit   View   Favorites   Tools   Help

Address   http://users.california.com/~csuppes/NFL/DallasCowboys/index.htm

Texas Stadium

Allen Kaye of Allsport

Administrative   Stadium Resources

Done

In addition to giving detailed attendance records, this **Texas Stadium** site also provides links to information on the Dallas Cowboys' former stadium, the Cotton Bowl, and the new stadium that is on the drawing board.

known as RealGrass serves as the playing field. The Cowboys once played on the artificial Texas Turf, but the hard surface took its toll on players' knees and joints. One fan referred to it as "fuzzy cement."[2] The team switched to the cushier turf in 2002.

Many fans love Texas Stadium for its simplicity and tradition. However, the venue lacks the architectural beauty of modern stadiums. Wrote one fan, "Texas Stadium is old and ugly. Pure 70's with no attempt to make it any better looking. No glass, no brick, no stucco, no nothing. Just concrete brutalism."[3] A new Cowboys stadium is in the works. Until then, fans will have to cope with the architecture and enjoy the game.

Game Day

In Irving, all roads lead to Texas Stadium. The structure is surrounded by four major highways, although traffic bunches up badly near game time. Ticket prices are among the cheapest in the NFL— although still rather pricey. In 2006, standard tickets cost forty-eight dollars apiece.

Part of the fun of the NFL experience is tailgating in the parking lot before games. Cowboys fans are allowed to bring grills and fry up everything from burgers to fajitas. Many early arrivals visit the Corral, an enormous tent outside Gate 8. From three hours before game time until two hours after, the Corral is one big party. Three dollars gets you in the tent, where music, beverages, and food await. A favorite is the individually sized made-to-order pizzas from Piezo, a much-loved pizza chain in Dallas. Fans often meet local celebrities in the Corral, including former Cowboys players.

Fans make sure to reach their seats in time for the action. Fireworks erupt during player introductions, and emotions are sky-high upon kickoff. The world-famous Dallas Cowboys Cheerleaders perform throughout the game, as does Rowdy the Mascot.

Dressed like a cowboy, while wearing a Cowboys jersey, Rowdy speeds onto the field on his four-wheeler. He tosses T-shirts into the stands and displays signs, such as "Let's Go Cowboys." Sometimes he will poke a little fun at the opposing team. (He really lets loose during training camp. When the heat approaches 100°F, he runs around spraying young fans with water guns.)

Fans dread the endless lines at the Texas Stadium restrooms. They also gripe about food prices, which actually are not as high as at other NFL stadiums. Hungry fans can order a Red

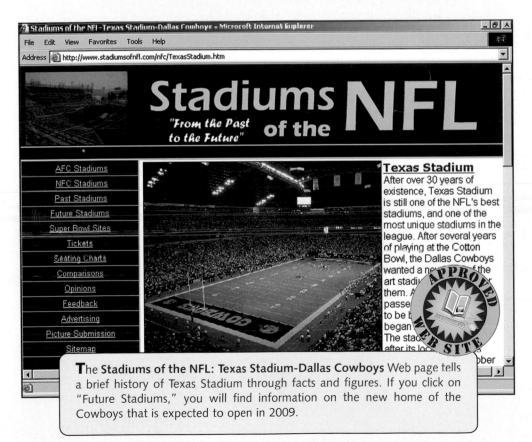

The **Stadiums of the NFL: Texas Stadium-Dallas Cowboys** Web page tells a brief history of Texas Stadium through facts and figures. If you click on "Future Stadiums," you will find information on the new home of the Cowboys that is expected to open in 2009.

Baron's mini pizza for $5.50, or a Texas-sized bowl of "Super Bowl Nachos" for $7.50. In the Lone Star State, the soda of choice is Dr Pepper.

For those with more money to spend, the stadium includes forty specialty shops. Since the 1970s, memorabilia for America's Team has flown off the shelves. The Cowboys logo has been slapped on such items as hammers, fishing lures, dog collars, hair scrunchies, and window valances. Reebok even makes Cowboys football uniforms and cheerleader outfits for infants. They start 'em young in Cowboy Country.

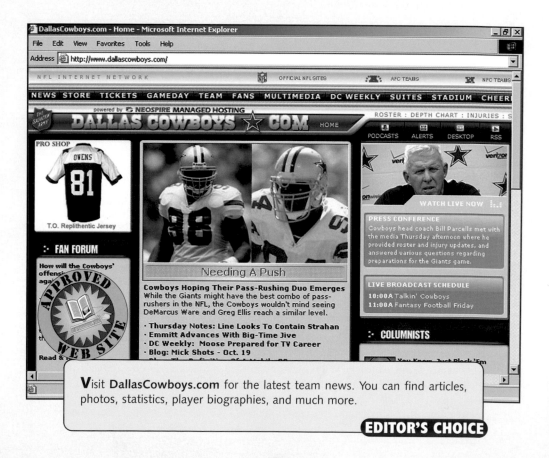

Visit DallasCowboys.com for the latest team news. You can find articles, photos, statistics, player biographies, and much more.

EDITOR'S CHOICE

➔ Following the Cowboys

As with all other NFL teams, Dallas games are broadcast on the national networks: FOX, NBC, CBS, and ESPN. However, some Cowboy diehards mute their TVs and listen to Brad Sham on the radio. For twenty-eight seasons, through 2006, Sham has been the "Voice of the Cowboys." The masterful play-by-play announcer was named Texas Sportscaster of the Year eight times—the maximum allowed.

During football season, the Cowboys dominate the sports sections of *The Dallas Morning News* and the *Star Telegram* (in nearby Ft. Worth). Fans can subscribe to *Dallas Cowboys Weekly,* the official newspaper of the Cowboys. They also can access the team's official web page. The Web site profiles each player on the roster. It also provides player statistics, team news, a history of the Cowboys, and a seemingly endless number of links. Over the next couple of years, the site undoubtedly will provide more and more information about the Cowboys' new stadium.

➔ A New Home on the Range

Since the early 1990s, most NFL teams have renovated their homes or built "megastadiums." Now it is the Cowboys' turn. In 2004, voters in nearby Arlington, Texas, approved a tax increase to help the Cowboys build a $650 million stadium. Public funds will provide $425 million, the Cowboys will contribute $150 million, and the NFL will chip in $75 million.

The new stadium should be spectacular. It will feature a retractable roof. In comfortable weather, the roof will be opened. In cold, muggy, snowy, or rainy weather, the roof will be closed. For the first time in decades, the Cowboys will play on real grass. The stadium will include seventy-five thousand seats. It also will feature extended decks in the end zones that could increase seating to one hundred thousand.

The stadium promises to be extremely lucrative for Cowboys owner Jerry Jones. Suite and seat revenue will skyrocket. Moreover, the stadium's

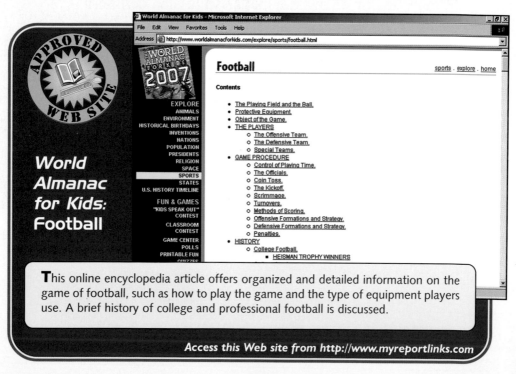

World Almanac for Kids: Football

This online encyclopedia article offers organized and detailed information on the game of football, such as how to play the game and the type of equipment players use. A brief history of college and professional football is discussed.

Access this Web site from http://www.myreportlinks.com

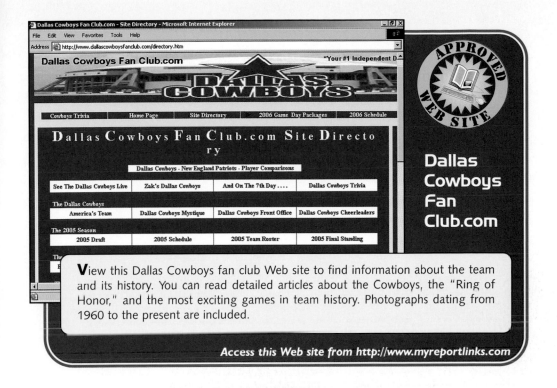

Dallas Cowboys Fan Club.com

View this Dallas Cowboys fan club Web site to find information about the team and its history. You can read detailed articles about the Cowboys, the "Ring of Honor," and the most exciting games in team history. Photographs dating from 1960 to the present are included.

Access this Web site from http://www.myreportlinks.com

Legends Square will be like the team's own shopping mall. Open year-round, the square will boast numerous shops and restaurants. Texans will also flock to the Cowboys Experience, an entertainment area for fans young and old. Reportedly, the Experience will celebrate the legacy of the Cowboys.

The new stadium is scheduled to open in 2009. Sometime after that, Jones hopes to host an event that has never been staged in the Dallas area: the Super Bowl.

▲ Bob Lilly (No. 74) is ready to pounce on Green Bay quarterback
Bart Starr in this action photo from the 1967 Pro Bowl.

RING OF HONOR

Many Dallas players have made the Pro Bowl or won the Super Bowl. But only a select few have been named to the Cowboys Ring of Honor. In addition to Tom Landry (coach) and Tex Schramm (general manager), only fifteen Cowboys have been enshrined in the hallowed RoH. These are their stories.

Bob Lilly

Only one man can be nicknamed "Mr. Cowboy," and the honor goes to Bob Lilly. One reason for this is because he came first. He was the first player the Cowboys ever drafted (1961), their first All-Pro, and their first Pro Bowl selection. Moreover, he was the initial member of the Cowboys Ring of Honor.

Lilly grew up in the town of Throckmorton, about three hours west of Dallas. He fulfilled his goal of playing college football in the Lone Star

State, earning All-America honors at Texas Christian. In the early 1960s, his most far-fetched dream came true. Dallas was granted an NFL team, and he was selected as the cornerstone of the franchise.

Lilly dominated at defensive tackle. He was huge for his time: six feet five inches, 250 pounds. Lean and fast, he could snatch ball carriers as they raced around end. All the while, he crushed offensive linemen like soda pop cans with his Herculean strength. "Let me tell you something about Bob Lilly," quipped a teammate at Texas Christian. "If I was as big and strong as him, I would charge folks just to live."[1]

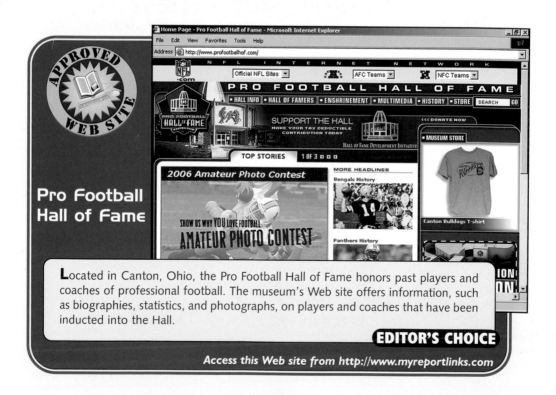

Pro Football Hall of Fame

Located in Canton, Ohio, the Pro Football Hall of Fame honors past players and coaches of professional football. The museum's Web site offers information, such as biographies, statistics, and photographs, on players and coaches that have been inducted into the Hall.

EDITOR'S CHOICE

Access this Web site from http://www.myreportlinks.com

Lilly was named to eleven Pro Bowls, including ten in a row. He also was named to the NFL's 75th Anniversary Team. In 1980, he was inducted into the Pro Football Hall of Fame. Not surprisingly, he was the first Cowboy to be so honored.

Don Meredith

Cowboys coach Tom Landry believed in the traditional values of honor and respect. He would have cringed if he had heard his quarterback greet United States Vice President Spiro Agnew. "Glad to meet ya, Mr. Vice Prez," Don Meredith reportedly said. "Love ya, but didn't vote for ya."[?]

Yes, "Dandy Don" was a bit of a free spirit. On the field, though, few questioned his grit, determination, and leadership. Born in Mount Vernon, Texas, he starred at Southern Methodist University in Dallas before becoming an original Cowboy in 1960. Gradually, he took over as Dallas's starting quarterback. From 1965 through 1968, he led the Cowboys to the playoffs each season. Twice he took his team to the NFL Championship Game.

Meredith's overflowing self-confidence served him well on the gridiron. He is the only Dallas QB to throw for 5 touchdowns in a game three times. He once compiled three 300-yard passing games in one season. In 1966, he fired 24 touchdown passes and was named the NFL Player of the Year.

89

In the 1970s and 1980s, Meredith worked on ABC's *Monday Night Football* as a color commentator. Folksy and funny, Meredith often broke into song during the fourth quarter. When the outcome of the game was no longer in doubt, he sang "Turn out the lights, the party's over. . . ."[3] In 1976, Meredith became the first of three quarterbacks enshrined in the Cowboys Ring of Honor.

➲ Don Perkins

Any Cowboys fan can tell you the three most prolific running backs in team history: Emmitt Smith, Tony Dorsett, and Don Perkins. On the club's all-time rushing list, they rank first through third, respectively. They are also the only running backs in the Cowboys Ring of Honor.

Perkins was an original Cowboy. In fact, the team signed him before it was granted an NFL franchise. In 1961, his first year in the league, Perkins ran for 815 yards. "I was small [5'10"]," he said, "but I was one that was afraid. When you're scared, you can run real fast." He may have run scared, but he earned the NFL Rookie of the Year Award.[4]

In 1962, Perkins amassed 945 yards, the most of his career. He played eight seasons in the NFL, all with Dallas, topping 600 yards every year. Late in his career, he switched to fullback, where he became an exceptional blocker. Overall, Perkins was named to six Pro Bowls and rushed for 42 touchdowns. When he retired after the 1968 season, he ranked fifth in NFL history with 6,217 rushing yards.

⊜ Chuck Howley

What a waste, sports fans must have thought. At West Virginia University, Chuck Howley had excelled in not just one, but five sports. He starred as a sprinter and wrestler. He competed in gymnastics, and he won the Southern Conference one-meter diving championship. Most of all, he shone on the football field, and in 1958 the Chicago Bears drafted him in the first round. But Howley played just two seasons for the Bears before retiring with a knee injury. Down on his luck, he took a job at a gas station.

In 1961, Howley attempted a comeback with the Cowboys, and his knee held up all year. Little did he know that he would toil for fourteen seasons with Dallas.

An outside linebacker, Howley possessed the quickness to haul down halfbacks on sweeps toward the sideline. "Sometimes we allow certain people like Chuck or Bob Lilly to vary from our defensive pattern," said Cowboys coach Tom Landry. "People like Chuck can often do this and get away with it because of their outstanding athletic ability."[5]

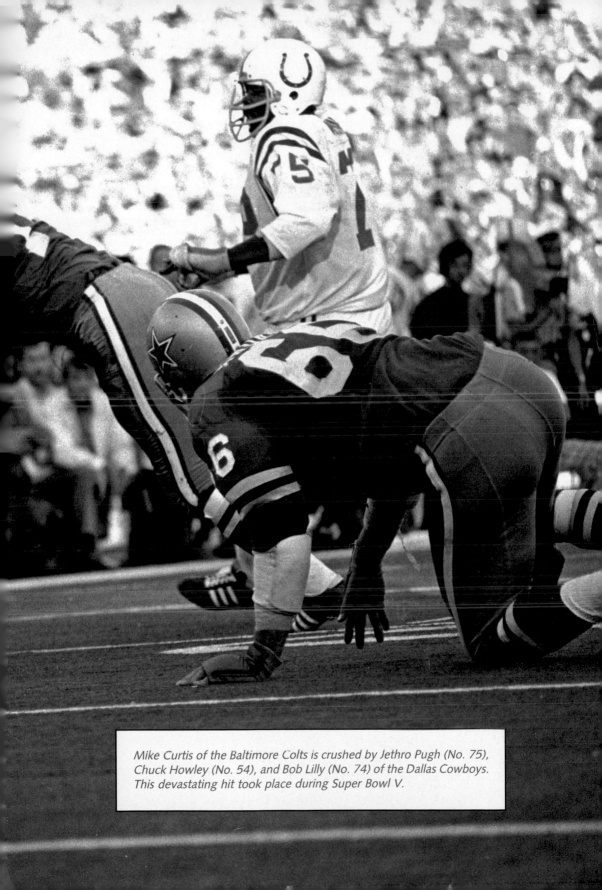

Mike Curtis of the Baltimore Colts is crushed by Jethro Pugh (No. 75), Chuck Howley (No. 54), and Bob Lilly (No. 74) of the Dallas Cowboys. This devastating hit took place during Super Bowl V.

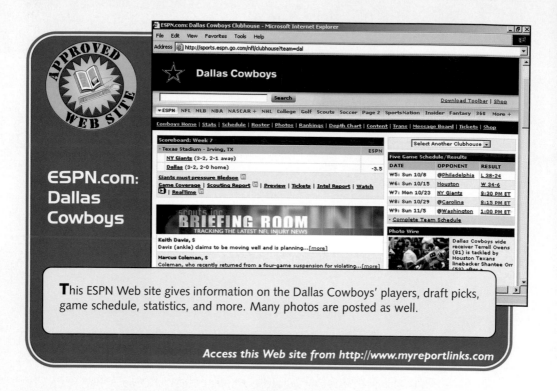

ESPN.com:
Dallas
Cowboys

This ESPN Web site gives information on the Dallas Cowboys' players, draft picks, game schedule, statistics, and more. Many photos are posted as well.

Access this Web site from http://www.myreportlinks.com

Howley wreaked havoc all over the field. In his career with Dallas, he picked off 24 passes and forced 16 fumbles. Six times he was named All-Pro. The Cowboys lost Super Bowl V to the Baltimore Colts 16–13, but Howley intercepted 2 passes and recovered a fumble. He became the first defensive player, and first member of a losing team, to win Super Bowl MVP honors.

In 1973, he retired again. Only this time, no one needed to feel sorry for ol' Chuck Howley.

Mel Renfro

In 1963, Mel Renfro of the University of Oregon was considered the greatest halfback in college football. But as a pro, he would take a handoff only eight times. Coach Tom Landry believed that this sensational athlete would help the team more in the defensive backfield and on special teams. Renfro did not argue. He simply became perhaps the best defensive back and kick returner in Cowboys history.

As a rookie in 1964, Renfro ran wild. He led the NFL in both kickoff and punt return yardage. At safety, he snatched 7 interceptions. A year later, Renfro averaged 30 yards on his kickoff returns. He switched to cornerback in 1968, but Renfro remained a scourge to quarterbacks. In 1969, he paced the league with 10 pickoffs.

Year after year, Renfro remained a defensive terror. He played fourteen seasons in Big D, one shy of the team record. His ten Pro Bowl appearances rank second among Cowboys, trailing Bob Lilly's eleven. Renfro flashed his considerable skill at the 1971 Pro Bowl. He returned not one but two punts for touchdowns, earning the game's MVP award.

→ Roger Staubach

Throughout the state of Texas, the mere utterance of his name inspires reverence and awe: *Roger Staubach*. "He had an air about him," said Hall of Fame quarterback Sid Luckman. "You knew someone special was on the field."[6]

Leaping into the air, Mel Renfro (No. 20) and Cliff Harris of the Cowboys break up a pass intended for John Stallworth of the Pittsburgh Steelers.

As a junior at the Naval Academy in 1963, Staubach won the Heisman Trophy. The young quarterback dodged defenders like a halfback, and he possessed a powerful, accurate arm. However, his NFL future had to wait, as Staubach had committed to serve in the Navy for four years after graduation. Only the Cowboys were willing to wait that long. In 1964, they drafted him in the tenth round.

Staubach did not join the 'Boys until 1969, and he did not start for another two years. But from 1964 on, he studied the Dallas playbook and attended the team's training camps. By 1971, he was primed for greatness. Staubach threw 15 touchdown passes and only 4 interceptions that season, earning league MVP honors.

Captain Comeback

During the 1970s, Staubach led the Cowboys to six NFC Championship Games and four Super Bowls, winning two. His exciting scrambles earned him the inevitable nickname "Roger the Dodger." The press also dubbed him "Captain Comeback." Cool and courageous, Staubach led Dallas to twenty-three come-from-behind victories in the fourth quarter. In seventeen of those games, the comeback came in the final two minutes. Said teammate Billy Joe Dupree, "Roger never knew when the game was over."[7]

▲ *"Roger the Dodger" Staubach eludes the defensive pursuit. Staubach led the Cowboys to four Super Bowl appearances.*

Staubach paced the NFL in passing four times, and he earned six trips to the Pro Bowl. By the time he retired in 1979, he was the highest-rated passer in NFL history.

Lee Roy Jordan

In 1963, Lee Roy Jordan shared a bizarre association with President John F. Kennedy. JFK attended that year's Orange Bowl between Alabama (Jordan's team) and Oklahoma. Jordan played out of his mind that day, making an unbelievable 31 tackles. It was Jordan's final college game as well as the last that the president ever attended. In spring 1963, Jordan was drafted by the Cowboys. That fall, Kennedy was assassinated . . . in Dallas.

For fourteen seasons, Jordan anchored the Cowboys' "Doomsday Defense." He starred at middle linebacker, and for twelve of those years he was flanked by Chuck Howley and Dave Edwards. Those two outside linebackers covered the left and right sides of the field, leaving the heavy-traffic area to Jordan. Though only 210 pounds, Jordan racked up tackles by the dozens. With exceptional quickness and instincts, he pounced on ball handlers. He sacked quarterbacks and picked off passes over the middle.

In 1971, Jordan set a Cowboys record with 21 tackles in one game. He went on to set team marks for career tackles (1,236) and solo tackles

(743). He spearheaded the defense on three Super Bowl teams, and was named to five Pro Bowls. Jordan and Howley are the only linebackers enshrined in the Cowboys Ring of Honor.

➔Tony Dorsett

As a lad in Aliquippa, Pennsylvania, Tony Dorsett had nightmares that he would toil forever in the town's steel mills. Unlike his older brothers, Tony was able to run away from such a fate. He ran and ran and ran. And no one, it seemed, could catch up to him.

At the University of Pittsburgh, Dorsett became the first man in NCAA history to rush for 1,000

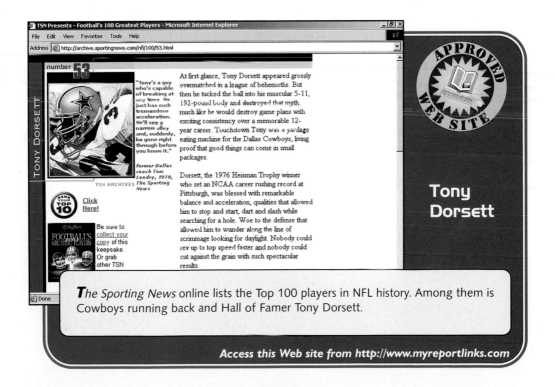

The Sporting News online lists the Top 100 players in NFL history. Among them is Cowboys running back and Hall of Famer Tony Dorsett.

Access this Web site from http://www.myreportlinks.com

yards in four straight seasons. In fact, his 6,082 career rushing yards set an NCAA record. Prior to the 1977 NFL Draft, Dallas traded four picks to Seattle for the Seahawks' No. 1 pick. With the first selection in the draft, the Cowboys chose Dorsett.

"TD" was as good as advertised. Though only five feet eleven inches and 185 pounds, he slithered through traffic and rocketed downfield. Dorsett sparked Dallas to the Super Bowl title as a rookie, and he became the first NFL back to rush for 1,000-plus yards in each of his first five seasons. Five times in his career he logged rushes of 75 yards or more, including an NFL record 99-yard burst.

In his career, Dorsett topped 1,000 yards rushing eight times. When he retired after the 1988 season, his 12,739 yards rushing trailed only Walter Payton's total in NFL annals. His career had not been a nightmare, but instead a dream come true. Upon his retirement, Dorsett noted: "I'm the second-leading all-time rusher and I played 12 seasons, when at one point I thought I would only play five. When I leaf through the pages of my scrapbook someday, I can smile about what I have done."[8]

Randy White

Cowboys safety Charlie Waters explained how he came up with defensive tackle Randy White's

▲ Randy White, known as *The Manster*, poses for a media photo on September 22, 1975. The inspired play of this ferocious defender earned him induction into the Pro Football Hall of Fame.

famous nickname: "Randy's charming, innocent demeanor transformed on game day to this despi-cable, nasty, destructive . . . well, 'monster.' From this unique combination of split personalities, I spawned the nickname 'The Manster'—part man, part monster, but perfect football player."[9]

In 1975, the Cowboys selected White with the No. 2 overall pick in the NFL Draft. He played line-backer his first two seasons before settling in at defensive tackle. Powerful and ferocious, White derailed running backs and flung quarterbacks to the turf. In 1978, he recorded 123 tackles and 16 sacks, earning the NFC Defensive Player of the Year award.

Randy White earned invitations to nine Pro Bowls. He became the first Dallas Cowboy to be named to the All-Pro team for eight straight seasons. In Super Bowl XII, he shared the game's MVP Award with cornerback Harvey Martin. He played fourteen seasons with the Dallas Cowboys, earning induction into the Pro Football Hall of Fame.

Bob Hayes

In a game against the Cowboys, Washington line-backer Sam Huff called a blitz. Cornerback Jim Shorter strongly objected. Why? "Because that means I'm covering Bob Hayes," Shorter told Huff, "and I can't cover Bob Hayes."[10]

Nobody could. He was, after all, the "World's Fastest Human."

In 1964, the Cowboys drafted Hayes out of Florida A&M, even though they knew he would not play football that fall. Hayes competed in the Summer Olympics in Tokyo. He not only won the gold medal in the 100-meter dash, but he also tied the world record.

Bullet Bob

Early in the Cowboys' 1965 season, all eyes were focused on Hayes. Sure, he could streak down the sidelines, but could he catch the pigskin? "Bullet Bob" proved himself in his very first game. He caught one pass for 37 yards. On another play, he raced 45 yards for a score.

Hayes, in fact, proceeded to revolutionize the NFL. No one could cover him one-on-one, so teams relied on newly created zone defenses to contain him. Hayes was so successful as a rookie (1,003 yards receiving) that he inspired other teams to draft speed-burner receivers.

Hayes enjoyed his greatest season in 1966. He caught 64 passes for 1,232 yards and scored 13 touchdowns. In one game, he amassed 246 yards receiving, including 95 on one play. In his first four seasons, Hayes caught 212 passes for 45 touchdowns. That is one TD for every 4.7 catches—the best ratio ever for a receiver over a

▲ Bob Hayes competed as an Olympic sprinter before joining the Dallas Cowboys. Here, he is shown waving to the crowd after his induction into the Cowboys Ring of Honor on September 23, 2001.

four-year period. For his career, Hayes caught 71 touchdown passes and averaged an amazing 20 yards per catch.

⊝ Cliff Harris

It is difficult to discuss Cliff Harris without mentioning Charlie Waters. In each year of the 1970s, they manned the safety positions for the Cowboys. They developed a brother-like bond, and they became a dynamic duo in the backfield. Wrote Roger Staubach, "They had an uncommon, often unspoken communion that allowed each to adjust instinctively. Cliff and Charlie knew the scheme so well, that they even made up some new coverages *during* a game."[11]

Of their combined nine Pro Bowl selections, Harris earned six of them. Amazingly, Harris was never drafted. After toiling at tiny Ouachita Baptist, he signed with Dallas and won a starting job during his rookie season. Unlike other free safeties, Harris tried to do more than just pick off wayward passes.

"Captain Crash" sent messages to receivers with his bell-ringing hits. "If you step in front of a receiver and intercept a pass, he'll be a little upset," Staubach remembered Harris saying. "But if you blast him, turn his helmet around, then he'll be looking for you. . . . After a hit, I ask, 'Was it worth it?'"[12]

Cliff Harris's revolutionary style of play strengthened the Cowboys defense. In each of his ten years in the league, Dallas ranked in the top ten defensively. Harris played in five Super Bowls, and he was named to the NFL's All-Decade Team for the 1970s.

Rayfield Wright

Early in his career, Rayfield Wright helped the Cowboys as a backup tight end, defensive end, and offensive tackle. In 1969, Wright's third year in the NFL, coach Tom Landry inserted him at right tackle. Deacon Jones, a future Hall of Fame defensive end, was his first opponent. "The Deacon is big and strong and mean," the line coach warned Wright. "Well," replied Wright, "so am I."[13]

Wright was born into poverty in Griffin, Georgia. Yet through the guidance of his grandmother ("Big Mama"), he overcame the odds. At Fort Valley State, Wright garnered interest from the NBA as a six-foot six-inch, 255-pound basketball star. In 1967, Dallas drafted him in the seventh round.

During the Cowboys' glory days, Wright anchored the offensive line. He walled off defensive ends with his massive size and strength, and his quickness prevented defenders from turning the corner on him. From 1971 to 1976, "Big Cat" was

▲ Offensive tackle Rayfield Wright was big, fast, and strong. He opened holes
for the Cowboys running backs.

named All-NFL every year. He helped the Cowboys to five Super Bowls and ten division titles.

Said quarterback Roger Staubach, "Rayfield protected me in the same manner in which the Secret Service protects our nation's President . . . with vigilance. He was a self-sacrificing power-house both on and off the field."[14]

➔ Troy Aikman

College ball was like a field day for Troy Aikman. At UCLA, he completed 65 percent of his passes. His 41 touchdown tosses dwarfed his 17 interceptions. In 1989, the Cowboys made him the No. 1 pick in the entire NFL Draft. But, oh, did he take his lumps as a rookie.

Aikman was tossed around like a sack of laundry as the Cowboys finished 1–15. The physical abuse he absorbed included a concussion and a broken finger. Aikman expressed his amazement that quarterbacks could last more than a few years in the NFL.

Yet the Cowboys turned their fortunes around thanks largely to the determination of their quarterback. Aikman demanded ultimate effort, from himself and his teammates. He fired laser beam passes with remarkable precision. And he proved gutsy and courageous, overcoming ten concussions in his twelve-year career.

Aikman won three Super Bowls, earning MVP honors in Super Bowl XXVII. From 1992 to 1997, he made the Pro Bowl every year. He holds numerous Cowboy, Super Bowl, and NFL playoff records. Moreover, he won more regular-season games in one decade (ninety in the 1990s) than any other quarterback in NFL history.

Troy Aikman retired with 32,942 yards passing, the most in Cowboys history. He never would have believed it during his rookie year, but in 2006 he was inducted into the Pro Football Hall of Fame.

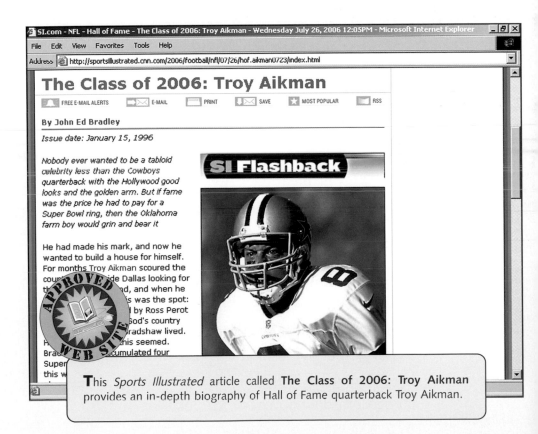

This *Sports Illustrated* article called **The Class of 2006: Troy Aikman** provides an in-depth biography of Hall of Fame quarterback Troy Aikman.

Emmitt Smith

As a young Cowboys halfback, Emmitt Smith answered to the nickname "Magic Man." He slipped out of tackles like Houdini, and he left defenders scratching their heads. "Magic," Dallas teammate Issiac Holt would ask, "are you going to disappear on someone today?"[15]

Smith had his own magic number: 100. Whenever he ran for 100 yards, the Cowboys almost always prevailed. In thirteen seasons with Dallas, and two with the Arizona Cardinals, he accumulated seventy-eight 100-yard games—an NFL record. In high school, he set the national record with forty-five 100-yard games.

Fast and powerful, Smith also possessed incredible instincts. "He seems to do something different every week," said Cowboys fullback Daryl Johnston. "He has a knack for hitting a hole at the right time; sometimes it's a quick move, sometimes he'll cut back. Every game you see one move that's better than the last time."[16]

Add in his remarkable durability, and it is no wonder he smashed numerous NFL records. Smith set career marks for both rushing attempts (4,409) and yards (18,355). He became the first running back with eleven consecutive 1,000-yard seasons and five straight 1,400-yard campaigns. No running back has ever matched his 166 regular-season touchdowns or 19 postseason TDs.

During the 1993–94 campaign, Smith earned MVP honors in the regular season and the Super Bowl. Yet he was even more prolific in 1995–96. That season, he rushed for a career-best 1,773 yards and an amazing 25 touchdowns—yet another NFL record.

Star running back Emmitt Smith follows the block of fullback Robert Thomas. In this game, Smith broke the all-time rushing record previously held by Walter Payton.

→Michael Irvin

On and off the field, Michael Irvin played hard. He wore gold jewelry and fur coats, and the front license plate of his BMW flashed his nickname: "The Playmaker." His partying clearly got out of

▲ Troy Aikman, Emmitt Smith, and Michael Irvin were often referred to as The Triplets because they were the three biggest stars on the Cowboys roster. The Triplets led the Cowboys to three Super Bowl titles in the 1990s.

hand. On multiple occasions, he was accused of or arrested for assault or drug possession. Irvin's sins at first dissuaded voters from electing him to the Pro Football Hall of Fame.

From 1991 through 1995, Irvin made the Pro Bowl every season while helping the Cowboys to three Super Bowl triumphs. During that stretch, he averaged 90 receptions and 1,419 yards per season. In his twelve-year career with Dallas, Irvin logged seven 1,000-yard seasons. In 1995, he set an NFL record with eleven 100-yard receiving games in one season.

A ferocious competitor, Irvin outfought defensive backs for position. He relished catching passes in the middle of the field, an area where he was vulnerable to bone-jarring hits. Irvin ran crisp routes, and quarterback Troy Aikman often connected with him on perfectly timed passes over the middle.

In 1996, Irvin pleaded "no contest" to drug possession charges. The NFL suspended him for five games. Irvin played until October 10, 1999, when he suffered a frightening neck injury. Michael Irvin was inducted into the Cowboys Ring of Honor in 2005 and the Hall of Fame in 2007.

Report Links

The Internet sites described below can be accessed at http://www.myreportlinks.com

▶**DallasCowboys.com**
Editor's Choice Browse the official Web site of the Dallas Cowboys.

▶**Official Site of the National Football League**
Editor's Choice Get the latest news from the official Web site of the National Football League.

▶**NFL History: Record & Fact Book**
Editor's Choice This NFL site features an in-depth at professional football in the United States.

▶**Super Bowl History**
Editor's Choice Learn about the history of the Super Bowl on this Web site.

▶**Pro Football Hall of Fame**
Editor's Choice Visit the official Web site of the Pro Football Hall of Fame.

▶**Tom Landry**
Editor's Choice An in-depth biographical look at "America's Coach," Tom Landry.

▶**The American Presidency Project: Remarks Congratulating the Super Bowl Champion Dallas Cowboys**
The president welcomes the Super Bowl Champions to the White House.

▶**The Class of 2006: Troy Aikman**
Read this *Sports Illustrated* article about Dallas Cowboys great Troy Aikman.

▶**Dallas Cowboys Fan Club.com**
Explore this Dallas Cowboys fan club Web site for information on the team.

▶**Dallas Cowboys (1960–Present)**
This site offers a detailed historical overview of the Dallas Cowboys.

▶**ESPN.com: Dallas Cowboys**
Visit the Dallas Cowboys Web site on ESPN.com.

▶**Football Glossary**
View a list of football terms on this Web site.

▶**Football Statistics Database: Dallas Cowboys**
View team statistics on this database Web site.

▶**The Helmet Project**
This Web site offers a catalog of football helmets, past and present.

▶**The Herschel Walker Trade**
Learn about the trade that helped build the Cowboys into one of the great teams of the 1990s.

Report Links

The Internet sites described below can be accessed at http://www.myreportlinks.com

▶**Murchison, Clinton Williams, Jr.**
A biography of the original owner of the Dallas Cowboys, Clinton Williams Murchison, Jr.

▶**NFLPlayers.com: Cowboys**
Find information on each of the current Dallas Cowboys.

▶**1967 NFL Championship: "The Ice Bowl"**
Read this article about the historic "Ice Bowl."

▶**1995 Dallas Cowboys Statistics**
A detailed look into the 1995–96 Dallas Cowboys.

▶**Official NFL Site for Young People**
This is the NFL's Web site for young football fans.

▶**Official Web Site of Emmitt Smith**
Running back Emmitt Smith's official Web site.

▶**The Official Web Site of Troy Aikman**
This is the official Web site of former Cowboys QB Troy Aikman.

▶**Parcells Officially Introduced As Cowboys' New Coach**
Read this AP article from January 2, 2003, about Bill Parcells signing on as the head coach.

▶**Professional Football Researchers Association**
The PFRA is an organization dedicated to preserving football history.

▶**The Rivalry**
Visit this Web site to learn more about the rivalry between the Cowboys and Redskins.

▶**Stadiums of the NFL: Texas Stadium-Dallas Cowboys**
This Web site describes stadiums of the NFL teams, past and present.

▶**Super Bowl XXVII**
An article about Super Bowl XXVII.

▶**Texas Stadium**
This site has facts, figures, and photos of the Dallas Cowboys' home field.

▶**Tony Dorsett**
Read a biography of former Dallas Cowboys running back Tony Dorsett.

▶***World Almanac for Kids:* Football**
This site offers general information about football.

COWBOYS

➔ Regular Season Statistics Through 2006—07

HEAD COACHES*	W	L	T	PCT
Tom Landry	250	162	6	.598
Jimmy Johnson	44	36	0	.550
Barry Switzer	40	24	0	.625
Bill Parcells	34	30	0	.531

Only includes career with Cowboys

QUARTERBACKS	Y	G	ATT	COMP	YDS	TD
Troy Aikman	12	165	4,715	2,898	32,942	165
Don Meredith	9	104	2,308	1,170	17,199	135
Roger Staubach	11	141	2,958	1,685	22,700	153
Danny White	13	166	2,950	1,761	21,959	155

RUNNING BACKS	Y	G	ATT	YDS	AVG	TD
Tony Dorsett	12	173	2,936	12,739	4.3	77
Calvin Hill	12	156	1,452	6,083	4.2	42
Julius Jones	3	37	721	2,896	4.0	16
Don Perkins	8	107	1,500	6,217	4.1	42
Emmitt Smith	15	226	4,409	18,355	4.2	164
Herschel Walker	12	187	1,954	8,225	4.2	61

STATS

WIDE RECEIVERS	Y	G	REC	YDS	AVG	TD
Bob Hayes	11	132	371	7,414	20.0	71
Tony Hill	10	141	479	7,988	16.7	51
Michael Irvin	12	159	750	11,904	15.9	65
Drew Pearson	11	156	489	7,822	16.0	48

DEFENSIVE PLAYERS	Y	G	PRO BOWL	INT
Cliff Harris	10	141	6	29
Chuck Howley	15	180	6	25
Ed "Too Tall" Jones	15	224	3	3
Bob Lilly	14	196	11	1
Mel Renfro	14	174	10	52
Deion Sanders	14	189	8	53
Everson Walls	13	185	4	57
Charlie Waters	11	160	3	41
Randy White	14	209	9	1

American Football League (AFL)—A pro football league that operated independently from 1960 to 1969. In 1970, the AFL merged with the NFL. Most of the AFL teams became the AFC, or American Football Conference. The teams that had already been in the NFL became part of the NFC, or National Football Conference. The winners from each conference meet in the Super Bowl.

ardent—Enthusiastic.

backfield—The players who line up behind the offensive line, usually the quarterback, halfback, and fullback.

bomb—A long, deep pass.

defensive coordinator—Coach responsible for a team's defensive players and strategy.

defensive line—The group of defensive players who line up along the line of scrimmage. It usually consists of the two defensive tackles and two defensive ends or a nose tackle and two defensive tackles.

dilapidated—Run-down or falling apart.

director of scouting—Person responsible for the scouts who recommend which players to draft or trade for. Scouts also look for weaknesses in the game plans of opposing teams.

Doomsday Defense—Nickname given to the Cowboys' stellar defensive unit of the 1970s.

dynasty—Adjective used to describe a sports team which has dominated its league for at least three to five consecutive years, either by winning championships or coming very close.

flattop—A close haircut, also called a buzz cut or a box top.

ingenious—Original or inventive.

midfield—The 50-yard line.

offensive coordinator—Coach responsible for a team's offensive players and strategy.

offensive line—The offensive players mainly responsible for blocking along the line of scrimmage. It consists of the center, left guard, right guard, left tackle, right tackle, and usually one or two tight ends.

onside kick—A kickoff during which the kicker strikes the ball so that it bounces along the ground and is difficult for the receiving team to catch. In this case, the kicking team hopes that one of its players can recover the ball before the receiving team. An onside kick must travel ten yards to be legal.

paydirt—A play that scores points, such as a touchdown or field goal.

picked off—Intercepted.

probation—A sentence in which a convict does not have to go to jail or prison. Instead, the criminal is allowed to go free, but has to meet with a probation officer to ensure that he or she has been well behaved.

rout—A blowout; when one team handily beats another.

salary cap—A set sum of money that teams are allowed to spend on players' salaries for each season.

showboat—Someone who is boastful and likes to show off, usually without giving the maximum effort to what he or she is supposed to be doing.

Super Bowl—Annual game held since the 1966 season to determine the best team in professional football.

turnover—When the offensive team loses possession of the ball either by fumble or interception.

Xs and Os guy—Someone good at coming up with football strategies or successful plays. When coaches chart out plays, usually the offensive guys are Xs and the defensive guys are represented by Os.

Chapter 1. Tension in Tempe

1. Michael Silver, "Special . . . Delivery," *SI.com,* February 5, 1996, <http://sportsillustrated.cnn.com/football/features/superbowl/archives/30/> (April 2, 2006).

2. Carl Moritz, "Forget 'Prime Time'—Brown is 'Right Place At The Right Time," *The Sporting News,* February 5, 1996, <http://www.highbeam.com/library/docfree.asp?DOCID=1G1:17920931&ctrlInfo=Round20%3AMode20b%3ADocG%3AResult&ao=> (April 2, 2006).

3. Paul Attner, "The Last of the Elites," *The Sporting News,* February 5, 1996, <http://www.supernfl.com/SuperBowl/sb30.html> (April 4, 2006).

4. Carl Moritz, "Forget 'Prime Time'—Brown is 'Right Place At The Right Time,'" *The Sporting News,* February 5, 1996, <http://www.highbeam.com/library/docfree.asp?DOCID=1G1:17920931&ctrlInfo=Round20%3AMode20b%3ADocG%3AResult&ao=> (April 4, 2006).

Chapter 2. America's Team

1. Richard Whittingham, *The Dallas Cowboys: An Illustrated History* (New York: Harper & Row Publishers, 1981), p. 32.

2. Ibid., p. 92.

3. Sam Blair, *Dallas Cowboys: Pro or Con?* (Garden City, N.Y.: Doubleday and Company, Inc., 1970), p. 380.

4. Whittingham, p. 110.

5. Peter Golenbock, *Cowboys Have Always Been My Heroes* (New York: Warner Books, 1997), p. 497.

6. "The 40 Greatest Games in Dallas Cowboys History," *Dallas Cowboys Fan Club,* n.d., <http://www.dallascowboysfanclub.com/history/bestgames.htm> (May 5, 2006).

7. "Super Bowl XIII," *Wikipedia,* n.d., <http://en.wikipedia.org/wiki/Super_Bowl_XIII> (May 5, 2006).

8. Whittingham, p. 189.

Chapter 3. Super Men Once Again

1. Peter Golenbock, *Cowboys Have Always Been My Heroes* (New York: Warner Books, 1997), p. 698.

2. Ibid., p. 752.

3. Ibid., p. 767.

4. Mike Fisher, *The 'Boys Are Back* (Fort Worth, Texas: Fort Worth Star-Telegram and The Summit Group), 1993, p. 12.

5. "There's No Getting Used to 0–4," *The Super NFL,* January 30, 1994, <http://www.supernfl.com/SuperBowl/sb28.html> (May 10, 2006).

6. Michael Knisley, "Mission Accomplished," *The Sporting News,* January 23, 1995, <http://www.highbeam.com/library/docfree.asp?DOCID=1G1:16218457&ctrlInfo=Round20%3AMode20b%3ADocG%3AResult&ao=> (May 11 2006).

Chapter 4. Ups and Downs

1. Arnie Stapleton, "Packers dump Cowboys into second half cooler," *Pecos Enterprise,* November 24, 1997, <http://www.pecos.net/news/arch97a/112497s.htm> (May 13, 2006).

2. Mark Wrolstad and Michael E. Young, "Landry memorial service features eclectic crowd with fond memories," *The Dallas Morning News,* February 18, 2000, <http://www.texnews.com/1998/1999/cowboys/service0218.html> (May 13, 2006).

3. "Farewell to football," CNN *Sports Illustrated,* April 9, 2001, <http://sportsillustrated.cnn.com/football/nfl/news/2001/04/09/aikman_ap/> (May 15, 2006).

4. Jaime Aron, "Parcells contructing Cowboys' blueprint," *Associated Press,* January 29, 2003, <http://www.insidecowboys.com/1998/2002/cowboys/parc012903.html> (May 15, 2006).

Chapter 5. The Masterminds

1. "Quotes by Tom Landry," *What Quote,* n.d., <http://www.whatquote.com/quotes/Tom-Landry/38163 Leadership-is-a-matt.htm> (April 24, 2006).

2. Cody Monk, *Legends of the Cowboys* (Champaign, Ill.: Sports Publishing, L.L.C., 2004), p. 23.

3. Peter King, "Monday Morning QB," *Sports Illustrated,* November 21, 2005, <http://sportsillustrated.cnn.com/2005/writers/peter_king/11/20/mmqb.week.11/3.html> (April 27, 2006).

4. Jean-Jacque Taylor and Todd Archer, "Parcells staying with Cowboys," *The Dallas Morning News,* January 6, 2006, <http://www.dallasnews.com/sharedcontent/dws/spt/stories/010706dnspoparcells.50298f0a.html> (April 28, 2006).

5. Mike Puma, "Parcells made struggling franchises into winners," *ESPN.com,* n.d., <http://espn.go.com/classic/biography/s/Parcells_Bill.html> (April 29, 2006).

Chapter 6. Welcome to Texas Stadium

1. "Texas Stadium," *gotickets.com,* n.d., <http://www.gotickets.com/scating_charts/football/texas_stadium.php> (May 16, 2006).

2. "Time to write a 9 digit check, Mr. Jerry Jones," *Epinions.com,* December 17, 2000, <http://www.epinions .com/sprt-review-3BBF-19726513-3A3DA92A prod4> (May 16, 2006).

3. "Home of the Dallas Cowboys," *SkyscraperCity,* April 28, 2005, <http://skyscrapercity.com/archive/index.php/t 206967 .html> (May 17, 2006).

Chapter 7. Ring of Honor

1. Cody Monk, *Legends of the Cowboys* (Champaign, Ill.: Sports Publishing, L.L.C., 2004), p. 49.

2. "SportByte Archives," *Bonesville.net,* n.d., <http://www .bonesville.net/SportByte/2005/0805.htm> (April 5, 2006).

3. Michael McCarthy, "Meredith to help turn out the lights for ABC's 'MNF' Finale," *USA Today,* December 21, 2005, <http://www.usatoday.com/sports/columnist/mccarthy/2005- 12-21 mccarthy-mnf_x.htm> (April 6, 2006).

4. "Don Perkins," *DallasCowboys.com,* n.d., <http://www .dallascowboys.com/history_roh_player.cfm?art=8> (April 6, 2006).

5. "Chuck Howley," *DallasCowboys.com,* n.d., <http://www .dallascowboys.com/history_roh_player.cfm?art=3> (April 8, 2006).

6. "Roger Staubach," *Famous Texans,* n.d., <http://www .famoustexans.com/rogerstaubach.htm> (April 9, 2006).

7. Ibid.

8. "Tony Dorsett had all the right moves and a brilliant NFL career," *Pro Football Hall of Fame,* n.d., <http:// profootballhof.com/history/release.jsp?release_id=789> (April 15, 2006).

9. Cliff Harris and Charlie Waters, *Tales from the Dallas Cowboys* (Champaign, Ill.: Sports Publishing, L.L.C., 2003), p. 107.

10. Monk, p. 80.

11. Harris and Waters, p. ix.

12. Ibid., p. viii.

13. "Rayfield Wright," *Pro Football Hall of Fame,* n.d., <https://www.profootballhof.com/hof/member.jsp?player_id =258> (April 12, 2006).

14. "Rayfield Wright," *rayfieldwright.com,* n.d, <http://www .rayfieldwright.com/wuf2.html> (April 12, 2006).

15. Leonard Shapiro, *The Dallas Cowboys* (New York: St. Martin's Press, 1993), p. 39.

16. Ibid., p. 42.

Buckley, James. *DK NFL Readers: Troy Aikman.* New York: DK Publishing, Inc., 2000.

Giglio, Joe. *Great Teams in Pro Football History.* Chicago: Raintree, 2006.

Golenbock, Peter. *Landry's Boys.* Chicago: Triumph Books, 2005.

Grabowski, John. *The Dallas Cowboys.* San Diego, Calif.: Lucent Books, 2002.

Harris, Cliff, and Charlie Waters. *Tales from the Dallas Cowboys.* Champaign, Ill.: Sports Publishing, LLC, 2003.

Jensen, Brian. *Where Have All Our Cowboys Gone?* Lanham, Md.: Taylor Trade Publishing, 2005.

Monk, Cody. *Legends of the Cowboys.* Champaign, Ill.: Sports Publishing, LLC, 2004.

Sham, Brad. *Stadium Stories.* Guilford, Conn.: Globe Pequot Press, 2003.

Shropshire, Mike. *When the Tuna Went Down to Texas.* New York: HarperCollins Publishers, 2004.

St. John, Bob. *Landry: The Legend And The Legacy.* Nashville, Tenn.: Thomas Nelson, Inc., 2001.

Stewart, Mark. *Dallas Cowboys.* Chicago: Norwood House Press, 2006.